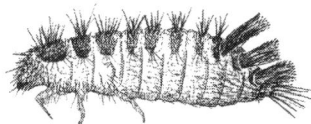   

GUIDE TO HOUSEHOLD AND WOOD INFESTING PESTS

By William H. Robinson, Ph.D.

Publisher: P.F. Harris
www.pfharris.com

© Copyright 2016

All rights reserved. No part of this book may be produced or transmitted in any form or any means, electronic or mechanical, including photocopying, recording or by information storage or retrieval system without permission in written form from the publisher.

Printed by CreateSpace, an Amazon.com Company

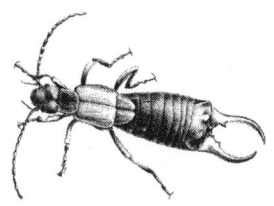

TABLE OF CONTENTS

CHAPTER	PAGE

1 - PEST INSPECTIONS – OUTDOORS 1

2 - PEST INSPECTIONS – INDOORS 19

3 - ANTS, BEES, WASPS 39

4 - BED BUGS, STINK BUGS, BOXELDER BUGS 55

5 - BEETLES 63

6 - COCKROACHES 81

7 - CRICKETS, EARWIGS, SPRINGTAILS 89

8 - FLEAS, LICE, SILVERFISH, PSOCIDS 93

9 - FLIES 97

10 - MOTHS 105

11 - TERMITES 111

12 - TICKS, MITES, SOWBUGS 117

13 - SPIDERS, CENTIPEDES, MILLIPEDES 123

14 - VERTEBRATES 133

PREFACE

This pictorial guide will help homemakers identify the pests that are commonly found around the outside and inside of their home or workplace. The objective is to provide practical information on pest biology and habits, and an accurate illustration of each pest.

This information and pictures in this guide book adds to the mission of PF Harris of providing homemakers with the most effective and economic material to control household and wood-infesting insects.

CHAPTER 1
PEST INSPECTIONS - INDOORS

The first step in controlling pests indoors is an inspection of the site to determine their location and abundance. This information helps determine the chemical and non-chemical control methods that can be used. Without a thorough inspection, control may be limited or short-lived, and time and material wasted. The initial inspection can provide information on conditions that are favorable to the existing pest or others that may move in later. Prevention is usually based on making non-chemical changes to the habitat and these are based on knowledge of the food and harborage requirements of insect and rodent pests.

STICKY TRAPS

The typical use for sticky traps indoors is to monitor or detect the presence of pests before and/or after chemical or non-chemical treatments.

- When placed close to pest harborages, sticky traps can remove and reduce infestations of insects or rodents that occur in low numbers.

- House centipedes, field crickets, and wolf spiders can be removed more effectively with sticky traps than they can with insecticide application.

Careful examination of the insects captured on sticky traps can provide information on the location of infested harborages. For example, the presence of female German cockroaches carrying an egg case indicates that an infested harborage is close to the trap. The presence of egg cases and the small nymphs that have hatched from them is another indication that an infested harborage is close. The abundance of males in a sticky trap is less indicative of a nearby harborage because males and large nymphs travel far from harborages in search of food.

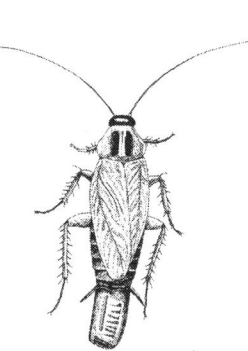

- Sticky traps that remain in place for long periods and have captured cockroaches, especially large species such as American cockroaches, may attract house mice. They may eat some of the insects trapped on the glue. Evidence of this will be only the legs and antennae of cockroaches and sometimes house centipedes.

GUIDE TO HOUSEHOLD AND WOOD INFESTING PESTS

TERMITE INFESTATIONS

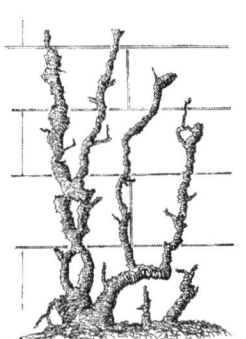
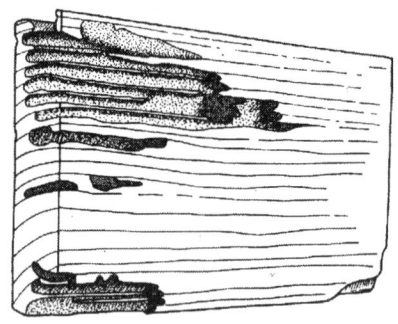

- **Subterranean termite damage** to structural wood is indicated by the presence of galleries in wood lined with soil. Typically the galleries follow the grain of the wood. Mud tubes may be found extending from soil to wood above ground. There is no frass, such as fibrous pieces of wood in the galleries.

The galleries may extend along the length of pieces of wood and to the wood above. When galleries are following moisture-damaged wood they may extend into wall framing and to floors well above the foundation. In severe infestations a large portion of the colony may be located in wood above ground. **See page 112.**

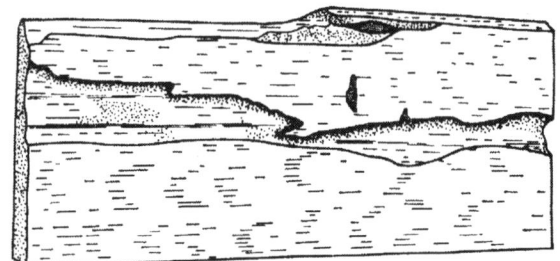

- **Drywood termite damage** is indicated by irregular galleries in the wood. The galleries do not follow the grain pattern of the wood. The colony is entirely above ground, there is no connection to soil by mud tubes. The sides of the galleries are not lined with soil, but are smooth. Colonies are generally small and isolated to a few pieces of wood.

The galleries of drywood may contain granular frass in the form of barrel-shaped pellets. The pellets are uniform in size and hardened, they can not be crushed by rubbing between fingers; they have distinct ridges. There may be holes (called kick-out holes) along some galleries where the frass pellets have been ejected from the gallery. **See page 114.**

FLOOR DRAINS

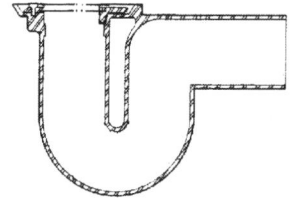

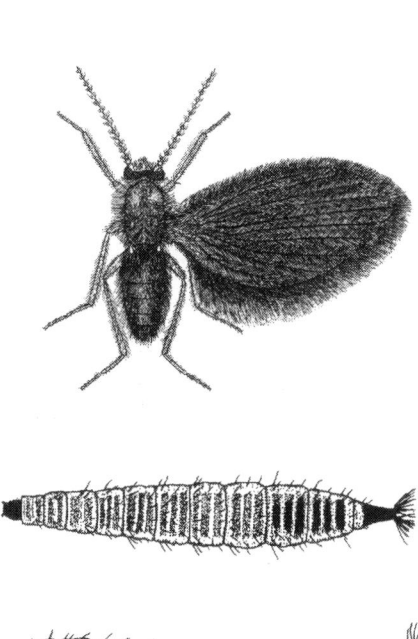

- **Moth fly** adults do not move far from their breeding site. The presence of moth flies is an indication that there are floor drains that are partially clogged with organic matter. The larvae are deep in the clogging material, and have the end of their body in contact with the surface. They breathe through the posterior end.

Control of drain flies in a clogged drain must include removing the organic matter. Larvae may crawl out onto the surface of the drain when the clog is close to the top, such as in shower drains. **See page 101.**

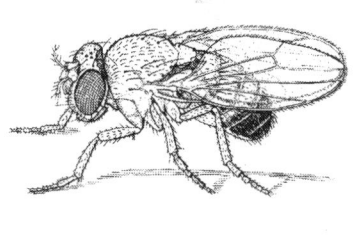

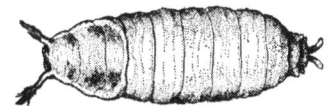

- **Dark eye fruit fly** adults usually do not remain close to their breeding site. They are usually found on walls and ceiling of the rooms that have infested drains. The larvae feed in accumulated organic material at the top of the drain and inside. They remain buried in the material when they feed and only the posterior end of their abdomen is in contact with the air. They breathe through the opening at the end of their abdomen. Larvae crawl away form the drain to pupate. **See page 99.**

FLOOR DRAINS Cont.

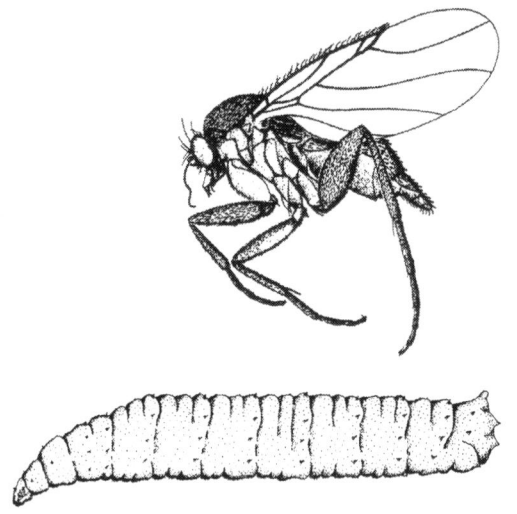

- **Phorid flies** are sometimes observed coming through floor drains or large number of adults seen around kitchen sink drains or other connections to the sewer system—whether it is a septic tank or standard sewer line. Adult phorids can be recognized by their erratic movement behavior and wing veins.

- **Phorid larvae** may be feeding on organic matter around the top of the drain cover, but are probably feeding on organic material from a broken sewer pipe.
  See page 100.

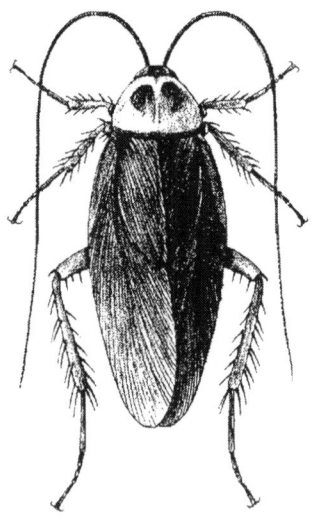

- **American cockroaches** are associated with floor drains in the basements of building, especially with drains that are connected to the sewer line or the below-ground storm drainage pipes. These cockroaches commonly infest storm sewers in major cities. Adults and nymphs can move from the sewer system through drain pipes that are not filled with water and then enter basements.
  See page 85.

Chapter 1: PEST INSPECTIONS – OUTDOORS

BATHROOM

- **Moth flies** are usually seen on the wall close to the breeding site of the larvae. In a bathroom, larvae may breed in organic material around sinks and toilets, and in the clog of hair and debris in the shower stall. **See page 101.**

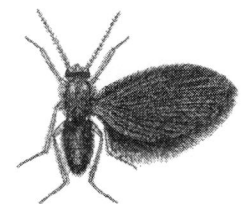

- **Phorid flies** can occur in bathrooms, but they are not usually breeding in drains. The larvae of these flies feed in the rich organic matter associated with a broken or damaged sewer pipe. If large numbers are found, check the sewer line or septic tank. **See page 100.**

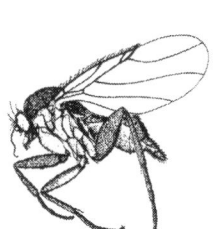

- **Carpenter ants** are associated with moisture-damaged wood, which they prefer to use as a nest site. Check the wood around and under the bath tub or shower. Acrobat ants may also occur in this location, they also nest in moisture-damaged wood. **See page 43.**

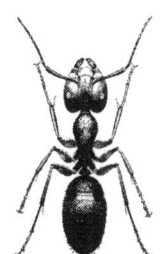

- **Psocids** are associated with high humidity conditions. These microscopic insects are sometimes found around the fixtures on the sink or tub. They may be breeding in organic material and mold on walls and cabinets. **See page 96.**

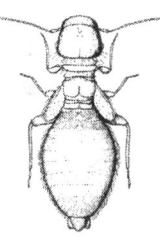

- **Carpet beetle** larvae can be found in bathroom closets, and sometimes climbing the wall. They feed on a variety of organic material, check for leather and food scraps. **See pages 75, 76.**

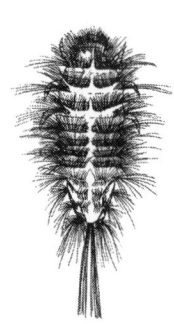

 GUIDE TO HOUSEHOLD AND WOOD INFESTING PESTS

BATHROOM Cont.

- **Rats and mice** are not usually found in bathrooms, but they can be attracted to moisture or have access through a crawl space below. Mice can become trapped in bath tubs, the sides are too smooth and they are not able to get out once they fall in. **See pages 134 - 137.**

- **Wolf spiders** are found in bathrooms because of the moisture and the lights may attract insects they can prey on. Place traps against a wall in open areas. **See page 128.**

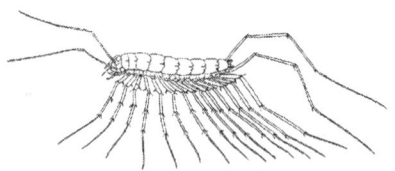

- **House centipedes** are often seen on bathroom walls and floor; they are searching for insects and spiders to feed on. They are often captured in sticky traps placed in cabinets and against baseboards. **See page 131.**

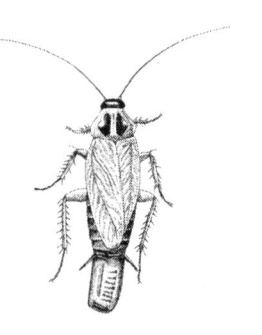

- **German cockroaches** can occur in bathrooms in houses or apartments that have a severe infestation. The bathroom may not offer food, but provides harborage and humidity. If females carrying an egg case are trapped in the bathroom, it indicates there is an infested harborage nearby. **See page 82.**

- **Silverfish** are in bathrooms because of the humidity and the potential of finding food. They feed on microscopic mold and organic material in cracks and crevices. **See pages 95, 96.**

Chapter 1: PEST INSPECTIONS – OUTDOORS

CLOTHING AND FABRIC

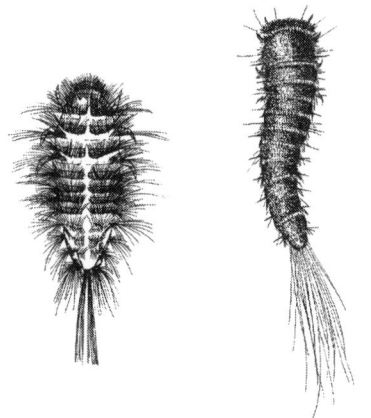

- **Holes in fabric** may indicate feeding by carpet beetle larvae, and clothes moth caterpillars. These insects attack natural fibers, such as wool and silk; they do not feed on cotton. Holes in cotton fabric may be caused by the teeth of the zipper on a garment hooking into a thread during washing.

- **Carpet beetle** larvae may be seen on fabric, or in closets or boxes that contain wool, silk, or furs. Sometimes only the cast skins of the larvae can be found along the edge of drawers or closets. **See pages 75, 76.**

- **Carpet beetle** adults are often found in the glass bowl of light fixtures in rooms that have an infestation; this may be the only sign that these beetles are present. Check for damage on natural fiber clothing, leather, and furs. **See pages 75, 76.**

- **Clothes moth** adults are not usually seen in closets or rooms that have an infestation. These moths are small and do not naturally fly to lights. It is the caterpillar stage of cloths moth species that damage fabric and other organic material. **See page 108.**

- **Silverfish** eat protein-based material indoors. Their damage to fabric is usually associated with fabric that has food stains or food material in the weave. Silverfish eat food stain material and damage the fabric in the process. breaks. **See pages 95, 96.**

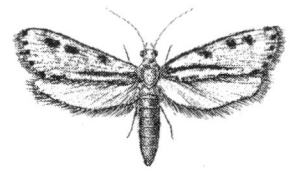

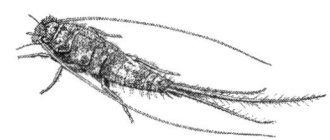

GUIDE TO HOUSEHOLD AND WOOD INFESTING PESTS

KITCHEN CABINETS

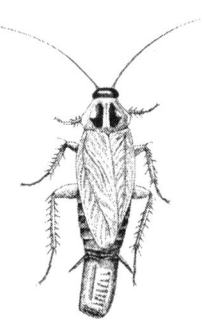

- **German cockroaches** can occur in and around kitchen cabinets, under sinks, and in food storage closets. Females carry their egg case for about 28 days and deposit it in crevices in cabinets. **See page 82.**

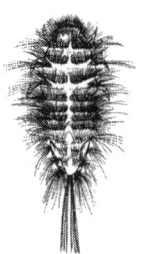

- **Carpet beetle** larvae infest a variety of food materials, including spices and dry pet food. Evidence of an infestation may be a large number of cast larval skins on shelves. **See pages 75, 76.**

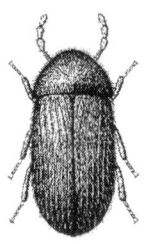

- **Cigarette and Drugstore beetles** are common in household food cabinets. Larvae feed on seeds, nuts, beans, spices, yeast, dried insects, fish, vegetables, flour, meal, and tobacco. The drugstore beetle also attacks leather and food stained fabric. **See page 71.**

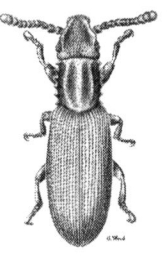

- **Sawtoothed grain beetle** is a common pest of flour and cereal products. These are the small beetles found in boxes of noodles and flour. Adults and larvae can be found in cracks and crevices in cabinets. **See page 72.**

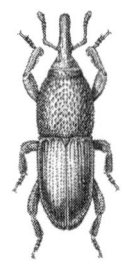

- **Rice weevils** are found infesting nuts, cereals, and cereal products such as macaroni, cake flour, and rice products. These are small beetles and may not be noticed until the infestation is severe. **See page 73.**

KITCHEN CABINETS Cont.

- **Indian meal moth** adults may remain close to the infested site, but may also be found in locations far from the kitchen. These distinctly marked moths remain inactive during the day and fly in early evening. **See page 106.**

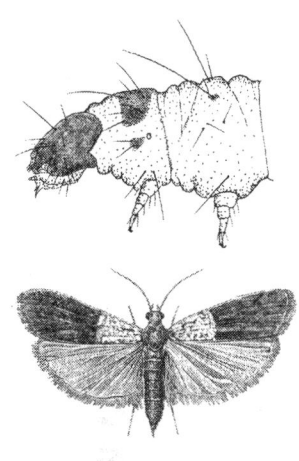

- **Indian meal moth** caterpillars remain in the infested food material until full grown, then they move away to pupate. Caterpillars can be found crawling on walls and the ceiling away from the infested site. They are sometimes considered maggots when they are crawling on kitchen counters. **See page 106.**

- **Psocids** are found in cereal products and flour. They are almost microscopic and may be unnoticed until the infestation is severe. They can be found in cracks and crevices in cabinets and sometimes on counters. **See page 96.**

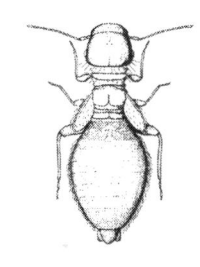

- **Pharaoh ants and Thief ants** are about the same size and shape, and they infest similar materials. Both species will forage widely indoors. **Pharaoh ants** typically have numerous small or satellite colonies scattered through a structure. **Thief ants** have similar habits. Both species feed on high-protein materials in kitchens and elsewhere. **See page 45.**

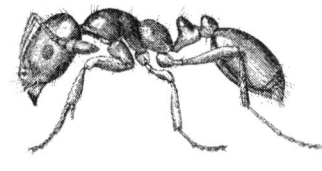

- **Mouse** droppings may be found in cabinets and on kitchen counters. In fall and early winter these droppings may be from deer mice, during other times of the year the droppings may be from house mice. **See pages 137.**

 GUIDE TO HOUSEHOLD AND WOOD INFESTING PESTS

BEDROOM

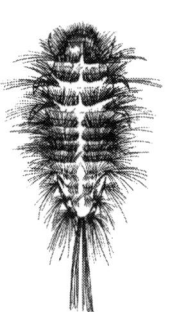

- **Carpet beetle larvae** or the cast skins of larvae are commonly found in bedroom closets and dresser drawers. The larvae feed on a variety of organic material, including leather and natural fibers. Larvae can molt many times and produce large number of cast skins which gives the impression of a severe infestation. **See pages 75, 76.**

- **Carpet beetle adults** are common in spring, at other times of the year the adults are not active. When large numbers of adults are found in light fixtures or other areas, it indicates that mice have cached food and it is infested with these beetles. **See pages 75, 76.**

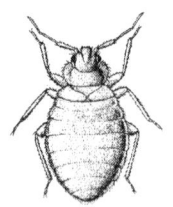

- **Bed bugs** can be detected using sticky traps. Adults and nymphs will crawl into traps that are placed along the baseboard under beds and behind and under furniture. **See page 56.**

- **Wolf spiders** are active at night when they search for insects and other spiders as food. They can be captured in sticky traps placed along baseboards, under beds, and dressers. **See page 128.**

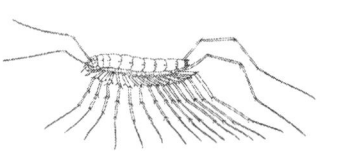

- **House centipedes** are often found in bedrooms where they are searching for insects and spiders as food. They are primarily nocturnal, and they move quickly on walls and ceilings. They can be captured in sticky traps placed along baseboards. **See page 131.**

- **House spiders** build webs in corners close to the floor and will move along baseboards, beneath beds, and in closets. They are frequently captured on sticky traps placed in corners. **See page 124.**

BASEMENT

- **Pine sawyer** damage may be seen in attic rafters and framing, and also in exposed floor joists in crawl spaces. These are never active infestations. **See page 67.**

- **Anobiid powderpost beetle** holes may be seen in attic timbers, but it is most common in exposed floor joists in crawl spaces. Frass may spill from emergence holes long after the infestation has died out. **See page 65.**

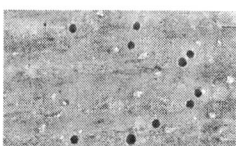

- **Pine bark beetle** damage may be found in attics and crawlspace timber that has a small amount of bark remaining on the pieces. These infestations do not remain active in structural wood. **See page 65.**

- **Termite tubes** may be visible in crawl spaces. They are typically against the foundation wall. Tubes extend from the ground to wood above, such as floor joists or the sill plat at the top of the foundation. **See pages 112 - 114.**

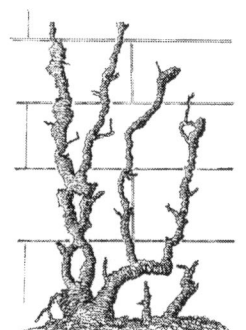

- **Cellar spiders** often occur in corners or between exposed floor joists. These can be large spiders with an unorganized web, but they are harmless. **See page 125.**

- **Woodlouse spiders** are common in fall, they often occur in sticky traps placed along walls. These spiders enter under doors and around basement windows from the mulch and turfgrass outside the foundation. **See page 126.**

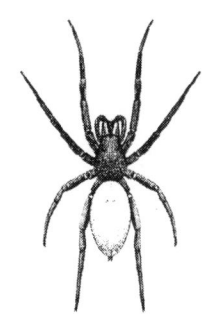

BASEMENT Cont.

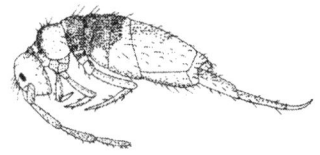

- **Springtails** require humid conditions; they can be numerous in basements that have moisture problems. They can occur near doors that open to the outside, and in shaded or dark corners of basements. **See page 92.**

- **Carpet beetle adults** may suddenly occur in large numbers, or be seen at lights or in light fixtures. This indicates food material stored in the basement is infested, or mice have cached food there and it has become infested. **See pages 75, 76.**

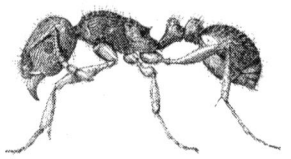

- **Pavement ants** will sometimes build nests at the top of the foundation wall, beneath the wood sill. Debris from the nest may include pieces of wood and give the appearance of a wood infesting beetle. **See page 42.**

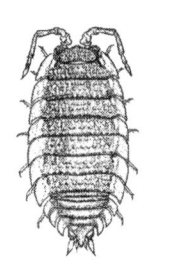

- **Pillbugs and sowbugs** may be seen dead a curled up on the floor, or crawling in moist locations. They come in from the mulch and vegetation surrounding the basement. **See page 122.**

- **Deer mice and house mice** often build nests in basements. Nests may be in corners where floor joists provide a protective location. **See page 137.**

- **Mouse droppings** may be seen along walls and on shelves, and on the top of the foundation wall, along attic rafters and framing, and also in exposed floor joists in crawl spaces. **See page 137.**

BASEMENT Cont.

- **Oriental cockroaches** occur in the basements of commercial buildings and large apartment buildings in urban areas. They may be outside the building perimeter during summer. **See page 82.**

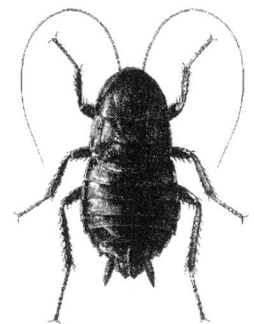

- **American cockroaches** infest the basements of buildings. The infestation may be linked to drain pipes that connect to the sewer system. Set sticky traps near drains. If captured cockroaches have been destroyed in the trap, it may have been done by mice. **See page 85.**

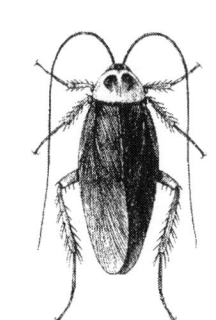

- **Wolf spiders** may be seen any time of year, but are most common in spring and fall. They come in from the perimeter where they live in mulch and vegetation. **See page 128.**

- **House centipedes** can survive in basements because of the available food, such as spiders and insects. Infestations are rarely large, sticky traps may be able to control them. **See page 131.**

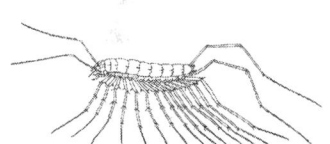

- **Field crickets** occur in small numbers in fall when they move to the perimeter of houses on cold nights. Sticky traps set in corners will help to capture these crickets. **See page 91.**

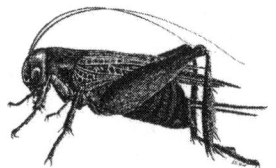

- **Camel crickets** may be found in dark basements that have a partial dirt-floor crawl space or high humidity. They can be captured in sticky traps with cockroach bait tablets. **See page 90.**

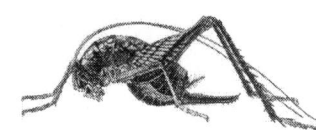

 GUIDE TO HOUSEHOLD AND WOOD INFESTING PESTS

DUMPSTER

- **Blow flies** are attracted to the odor of garbage in dumpsters; they will be active during the hottest part of the day. These flies follow food odors into restaurants near the dumpster. **See page 98.**

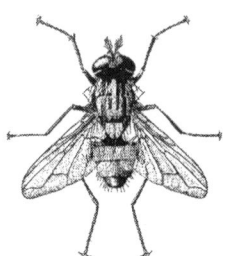

- **House flies** are attracted to the odor of garbage and females will lay eggs on exposed surfaces. Infestations can increase rapidly in summer when temperatures are high; adults will live for about one month, which results in large numbers in fall. **See page 100.**

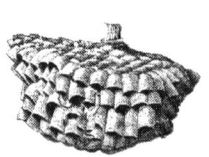

- **Umbrella wasps** often build nests in dumpster stalls. These sites give some protection and the wasps prey on the flies available. These wasps can be aggressive in the fall when the nests are large and there are many individuals. **See page 50.**

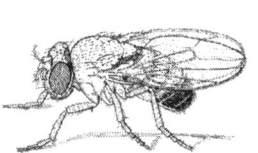

- **Red eye fruit flies** occur around dumpsters containing fruit and vegetable material. The maggots can survive in the humid conditions inside the dumpster, and the adults can fly short distances to kitchen doors. **See page 99.**

- **Norway rats** are common around dumpsters and dumpster stalls that are not kept clean. Rats may not be nesting at these sites, but simply coming there to feed at night. They move from the dumpster to buildings close to the stall. Rat dropping may be visible around the dumpster in the stall. **See page 135.**

Chapter 1: PEST INSPECTIONS – OUTDOORS

OFFICE – STICKY TRAP

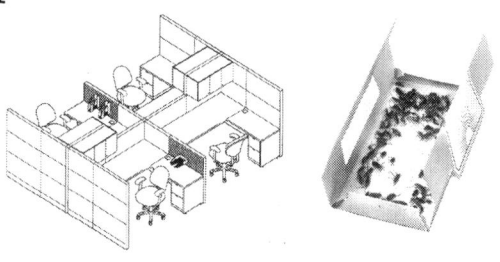

- **Pharaoh ants** and **Thief ants** occur indoors during all months of the year. These small ants build nests in many locations throughout a facility. They may be captured in only small numbers on sticky traps, but this is not an indication of a small infestation. **See page 45.**

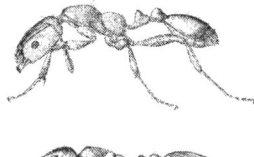

- **Wolf spiders** will be in sticky traps in spring and fall, especially traps placed near doors that open to the outside. Place traps along baseboards; in severe infestations a large number of spiders can be captured. **See page 128.**

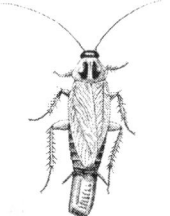

- **German cockroaches** may occur in small kitchens and employee break rooms, and where employees keep personal items. These cockroaches may be brought into the facility from outside in food material and personal belongings. **See page 82.**

- **House centipedes** are captured on sticky traps that are placed along baseboards. Infestations are usually only a few individuals and sticky traps can help remove them. **See page 131.**

- **Silverfish** occur in most office environments, but they are rarely present in large numbers. Sticky traps placed where the silverfish have been seen will capture some of them. **See pages 95, 96.**

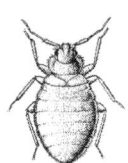

- **Bed bugs** occur in office environments because they can be brought from infested homes or other buildings. Sticky trap placed where they have been reported or where bites occur can help to locate infested harborages. **See page 56.**

KITCHEN - WINDOW TRAP

- **Blow flies** are common during the warm months, especially if there is a dumpster or garbage cans close to doors or windows leading to the kitchen. They fly to overhead lights during the day, but are attracted to light traps at night. **See page 98.**

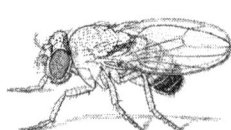

- **Fruit flies** are common in kitchens. The **red eye** fruit fly will be around fruits and vegetables, the **dark eye** on walls and ceilings. When infestations are high, these flies will be caught in light traps. **See page 99.**

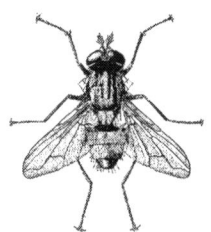

- **House flies** are attracted to the odor of food in kitchens and enter through doors and windows. Flies will move to light traps placed away from windows. UV light traps can remove most house flies from indoors, but there may be some that will not go to the trap. **See page 100.**

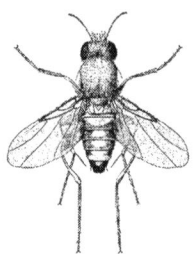

- **Phorids** are usually caught in light traps in small numbers, and it is usually the females that are attracted to UV light. The presence of these flies may indicate accumulations of rich organic matter; sewer lines should be inspected for breaks. **See page 100.**

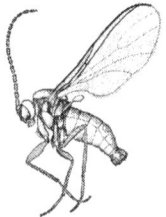

- **Fungus gnats** are often collected in light traps, sometimes in large numbers. They can easily move through window screens. Check potted plants for possible infestations. **See page 101.**

Chapter 1: PEST INSPECTIONS – OUTDOORS

FOOD STORAGE – STICKY TRAP

- **Larder beetles** crawl away from an infested location and be captured in sticky traps. To pinpoint the site of the infested material use a series of traps. **See page 77.**

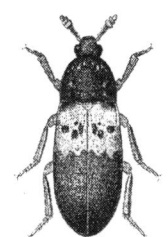

- **American cockroaches** are common in large facilities. They are active outdoors during the warm months and then move indoors during winter. Sticky traps can help locate the infested harborages, but the adults will forage far from a harborage each night. **See page 85.**

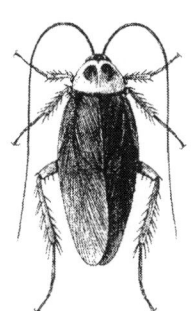

- **Flour beetles,** such as the Sawtoothed grain beetle, will move away from infested locations when the population becomes large. Set a series of sticky trap or pheromone traps to locate the infested material. **See pages 72, 74.**

- **Spider beetles** infest a variety of grain and meal products. They can become numerous when infestations persist for a long time. These beetles usually do not fly. Sticky traps with large number of these beetles may be close to the infested material. **See page 72.**

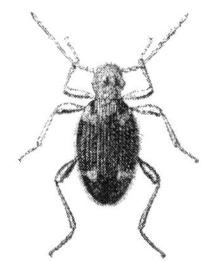

- **Pharaoh ants** and **Thief ants** may occur where food is stored. There are numerous places for the small nests or satellite nests produced by these species. Sticky traps may be helpful in locating a nearby nest, but the best control is to use baits and not liquid insecticide. **See page 45.**

 GUIDE TO HOUSEHOLD AND WOOD INFESTING PESTS

CLASSROOM - STICKY TRAP

- **Pharaoh ants** and **Thief ants** occur classrooms because of the opportunity to find nest sites and the potential of food scraps. Both species forage over a wide area and form small nests. Baits are the most effective control strategy. **See page 45.**

- **Wolf spiders** occur during spring and fall when they are most active looking for a mate and to get out of the cold. Sticky traps along baseboards and near door will help to eliminate many of these spiders. **See page 128.**

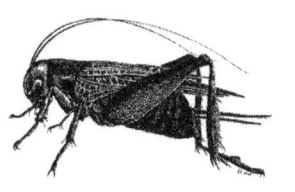

- **Field crickets** occur indoors during fall when the temperature begins to drop and the nights get cold. They enter around doors and windows. Sticky traps in dark corners help to eliminate these crickets. **See page 91.**

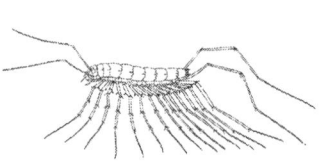

- **House centipedes** occur in classrooms because of the availability of food, such as spiders and insects. They are no threat to people unless they are handled, and they are difficult to catch. These centipedes are rarely numerous, but sticky traps can help remove them. **See page 131.**

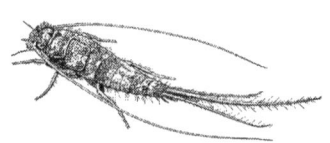

- **Silverfish** can survive in a classroom environment because of the harborage available and the abundance of food scraps. Populations can be reduced by the use of sticky traps placed along baseboards and in cabinets. **See pages 95, 96.**

CHAPTER 2

PEST INSPECTIONS - OUTDOORS

Plants, mulch, and piles of leaves outside houses provide harborage for pests. Earwigs, stink bugs, kudzu bugs, and spiders gather on the sunny side of houses and other buildings in fall. Several species of ants nest in soil along the perimeter of foundations, and workers from these colonies search for food indoors. Field crickets come to the foundation of houses when night temperature drops and they sense the heat at the foundation. They often move indoors around ground-level doors and windows.

Rodents and other animals often burrow or nest in the soil around houses, or under porches and decks attached to houses. Rat may burrow in the soil next to the foundation, and move indoors to search for food. Field mice enter houses in fall when temperatures drop and their natural food becomes scarce. Careful inspection is needed to locate the small openings used by mice and rats to enter houses. Removing debris and garbage around houses will reduce the presence of raccoons and skunks.

CONTROL METHODS

Controlling insects, spiders, and other pests that enter houses from the outside begins by treating their travel routes and their harborages. Many insects prefer to crawl along edges, such as the junction of the foundation and siding, or the edge at the bottom of a window frame. These sites often give them an entry point indoors. Treating these edges with insecticide will create a preventative barrier.

The foundation wall of houses retains heat at the end of the day in spring, fall, and early winter. This warm surface attracts crickets, earwigs, ants, and spiders, millipedes, and sometimes spiders. Treating the exposed foundation wall (up to a height of 3 feet) with insecticide can help to reduce the number of pests that come to the foundation and enter the house. Foundation walls facing the afternoon sun may have to be treated more often because exposure to the sun limits the residual activity of insecticides.

- Removing leaves, trimming bushes and shrubs, and limiting the thickness of mulch around the foundation of houses can help reduce the pests that move inside form these locations.

OVER-WINTERING PESTS

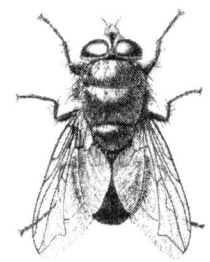

- **Cluster flies** gather on the sunny sides of houses and other structures in late afternoon in August and September. They move through cracks and crevices and enter the attic, wall voids, or the living space to spend the winter. **See page 99.**

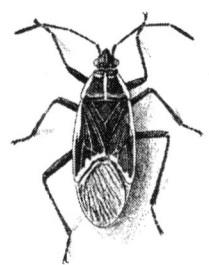

- **Boxelder bugs** gather in large numbers along the sunny side of building, foundations, and the base of trees in fall. They form large aggregations of nymphs and adults that will over-winter in protected locations. **See page 58.**

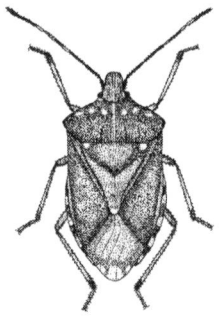

- **Stink bugs** gather as individuals on the sunny and/or warm sides of houses and other structures in fall. They crawl through cracks and crevices around doors, windows, and soffits to spend the winter indoors. **See page 57.**

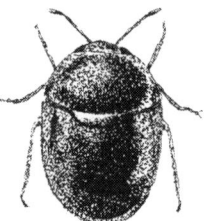

- **Kudzu bugs** gather as individuals on the warm and/or sunny sides of houses and other structures. They over-winter as individuals in protected locations. **See page 59.**

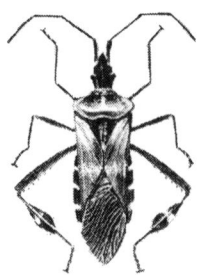

- **Western conifer seed bugs** come indoors in fall in small numbers. They may be under bark and come in with firewood. Once inside the adults become active and fly, they make a buzzing sound in flight. They do not bite. **See page 61.**

OVER-WINTERING PESTS Cont.

- **Asian ladybird beetles** gather in large numbers on the sunny and/or warm sides of houses and other structures in fall. They crawl through narrow openings to get inside the house or building, they sometimes over-winter in large masses outdoors. **See page 79.**

- **Elm leaf beetles** are associated with large, established elm trees; they often over-winter around the outside of building or in large number in the attics of houses. **See page 79.**

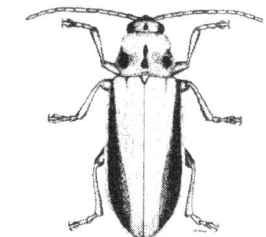

- **Yellowjackets** spend the winter in protected places, such as under loose bark of trees and firewood, they also over-winter in attics of houses that are close to their summer nest site. These are the queens that will start a new nest in spring. **See pages 51 - 54.**

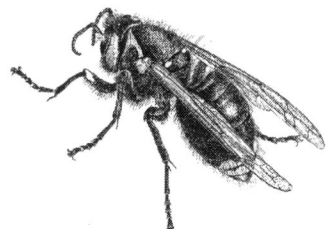

- **Umbrella wasps** over-winter in attics, usually near where their summer nest was located. They may be active in early winter (January) and fly to windows and lights in the living space. These are queens that will found nests in spring. **See page 50.**

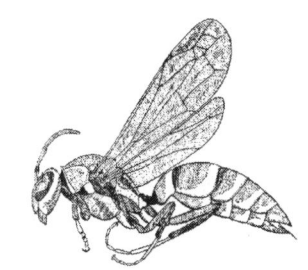

- **Mosquitoes** sometimes over-winter as adults, especially the species that breed around houses. These are females that select protected places to rest during winter; they usually do not bite during winter. **See pages 103, 104.**

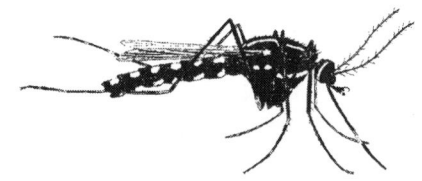

CRAWL SPACE AND ATTIC

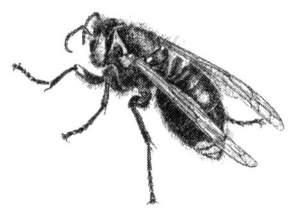

- **Yellowjackets** build nests in attics, usually close to an entry point, such as vents or louvers to the outside. The German yellowjacket commonly builds large nests in attics. **See pages 51 - 54.**

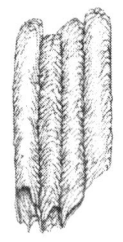

- **Mud daubers** build their mud nests close to openings, such as soffits and louvers at the end of gables, or close to the opening of a crawl space. Adult mud daubers are active in spring, they are not aggressive and usually do not defend their nest. **See page 49.**

- **Pavement ants** build nests at the top of foundation walls, between the foundation and the sill plate. Their nests often have wood shavings and can be mistaken for carpenter ants or wood-infesting beetles. **See page 42.**

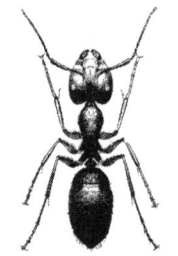

- **Carpenter ants** build primary or satellite nests in moisture-damaged wood in attics, typically in rafters that are below leaks around vent pipes or damaged roof shingles. **See page 43.**

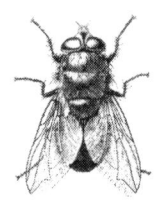

- **Cluster flies** will be in attics in fall and winter. They are generally not active during winter, and leave the attic in spring. There may be accumulations of dead flies in the attic. **See page 99.**

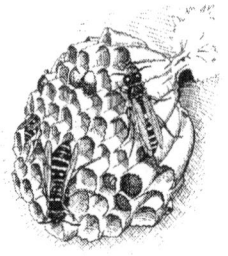

- **Umbrella wasps** build nests in attics, usually close to an entry point, such as vents or louvers to the outside. **See page 50.**

CRAWL SPACE AND ATTIC Cont.

- **Pine sawyer** damage may be seen in attic rafters and framing, and also in exposed floor joists in crawl spaces. These are never active infestations. **See page 67.**

- **Anobiid powderpost beetle** holes may be seen in attic timbers, but it is most common in exposed floor joists in crawl spaces. Frass may spill from emergence holes long after the infestation has died out. **See page 65.**

- **Pine bark beetle** damage may be found in attics and crawlspace timber that has a small amount of bark remaining on the pieces. These infestations do not remain active in structural wood. **See page 65.**

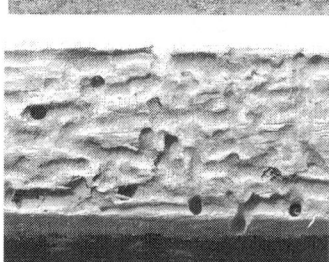

- **Termite** tubes may be visible in crawl spaces. They are typically against the foundation wall and extend from the ground to wood above, such as floor joists or the sill plat at the top of the foundation. **See pages 112 - 114.**

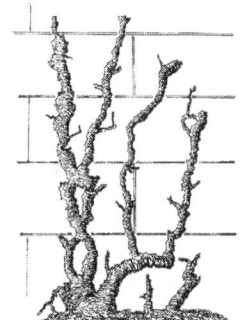

- **Black widow spiders** occur in crawl spaces, usually close to the entrance if it is a ground level. **Cellar spiders** also occur in crawl spaces, but they are harmless. **See pages 130.**

- **Camel crickets** occur in crawl spaces, usually when there is high humidity or water in the crawlspace. They will use wood, paper and other debris as a harborage. **See page 90.**

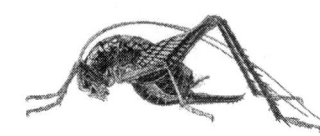

 GUIDE TO HOUSEHOLD AND WOOD INFESTING PESTS

OUTBUILDING

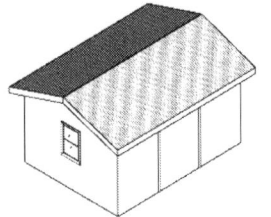

- **Black widow spiders** build their webs close to doors and inside in corners close to doors. The nests are usually close to the ground or floor. They are usually do not occur in large numbers inside buildings. **See page 130.**

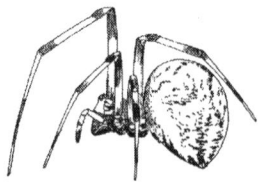
- **House spiders** will build webs between objects on shelves and equipment hanging next to walls. They can be very numerous in outbuildings, especially in late summer. **See page 124.**

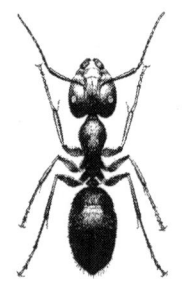
- **Carpenter ants** that are active in or around outbuildings may be a sign that there is a satellite colony in the structure. Moisture damaged wood at ground level or above may have a nest of carpenter ants. **See page 43.**

- **Umbrella wasps** will build their nests along the roof line of these buildings, or sometimes at the door or inside the door. In these undisturbed areas the nest can be large by late summer and fall. Wasps at this time will be aggressive and defend the nest site. **See page 50.**

- **Rats** build their nests close to the foundation of buildings. They are common when there are animal pens nearby or when animal food, bird seed, and other organic material is stored in the building. **See pages 134, 135.**

OUTBUILDING Cont.

- **Mud daubers** will build their mud nests close to door openings and also inside if there is a clear access from the outside. The nests are usually built high up and may be unnoticed. The wasps are active in spring and may be seen collecting mud or water nearby. They are not aggressive. **See page 49.**

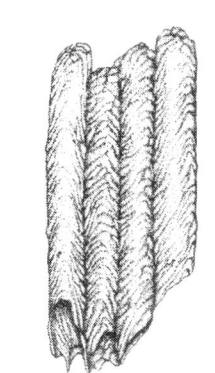

- **Carpenter bees** build their nests in spring. They select sites on sunlit sides of buildings, usually high off the ground. The entry holes in outbuildings may be hidden under eaves or along door frames. Females cut the entry hole and make the gallery. Males remain at the nest site and will threaten anyone approaching the nest. Males can not sting. **See page 40.**

- **Brown recluse spiders** will build their webs inside building and are often found in or around clothing materials in outbuildings. There may be several of these spiders inhabiting an outbuilding. **See page 129.**

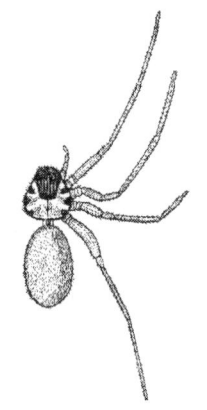

- **Subterranean termites** will infest wood that is close to the ground or in contact with the ground. Infestations may be linked to a large colony that is also infesting a nearby house, or a separate colony. **See page 112.**

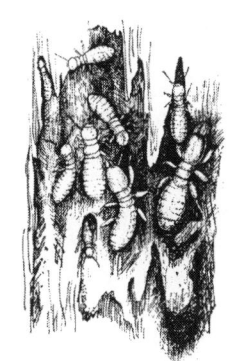

 GUIDE TO HOUSEHOLD AND WOOD INFESTING PESTS

FIREWOOD

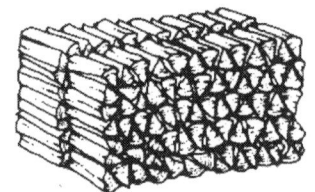

- **Black widow spiders** often occur around the edges of woodpiles, they may build webs in exposed sites between logs. In large wood piles there may be 2 or 3 females, but there will be a long distance between them. **See page 130.**

- **Carpenter ants** will build nests in logs in contact with the ground or close to the ground. There may be accumulations of fibrous frass in the end of some tunnels. Nests in wood piles may be a satellite for a large colony nearby. Foraging trails may extend to the house. **See page 43.**

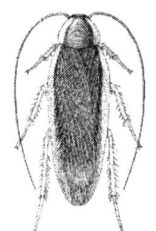
- **Woods cockroaches** may be found under the bark of hardwood and softwood logs; the nymphs are wingless and light brown. Adults will fly to lights at night in fall. **See pages 83, 87.**

- **Subterranean termites** may infest the logs in contact with the ground. The workers and soldiers may be found at ground level or in soil-lined galleries in logs. Infestation is wood piles may not extend to nearby structures. **See page 112.**

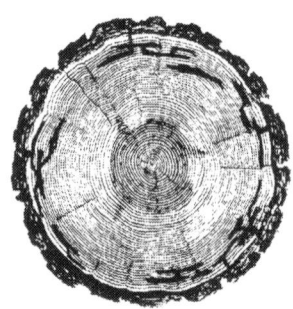 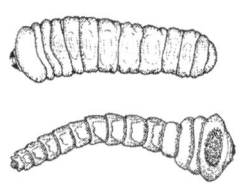
- **Longhorned beetle** larvae may occur at the surface or deep in logs that do not have contact with the ground. **Flatheaded beetle** larvae occur under the bark of hardwood and softwood logs. The sound of beetle larvae feeding under the bark of logs can be heard several feet from the woodpile. **See pages 67.**

WOOD-SHINGLE ROOF

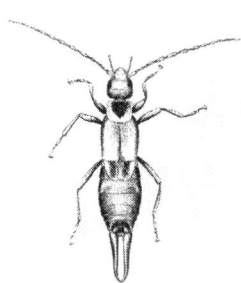

- **Earwigs** are good climbers and flyers, they can move from the tree branches contacting roof or fly to dark and moist habitat of weathered shakes. The shaded and north side of houses may have the most number of these insects. **See page 92.**

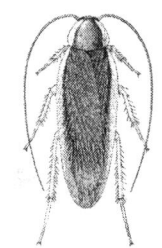

- **Wood cockroaches** can find harborage and breed between damp and decaying shakes that are in areas not exposed to sunlight. These cockroaches will come to lights at night. **See pages 83, 87.**

- **Carpenter ants** can establish satellite nests in the moisture-damaged shakes and the structural timbers below the shake the roof. Roof leaks that occur under shakes or along the flashing of a chimney or vent pipes can create favorable sites for these ants. **See page 43.**

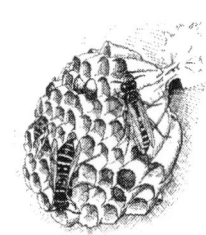

- **Umbrella wasps** can find suitable nest sites at the bottom edge of shake roofs, they can be out of sight. These nests can be origin of over-wintering females in fall and winter. **See page 50.**

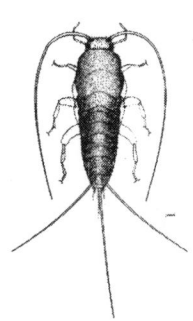

- **Silverfish** are common inhabitants of shake roofs because of the suitable harborage and available food. They can also occur in large numbers in the attics under these roofs. **See pages 95, 96.**

 GUIDE TO HOUSEHOLD AND WOOD INFESTING PESTS

TRASH AND DEBRIS

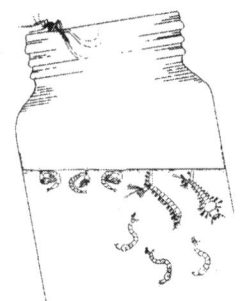

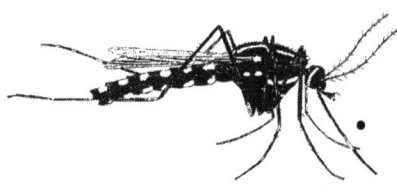
- **Mosquitoes: House mosquito and Asian tiger mosquito** will breed in standing water that collects in trash and debris. They can produce hundreds of adults mosquitoes from a small amount of water. **See pages 103, 104.**

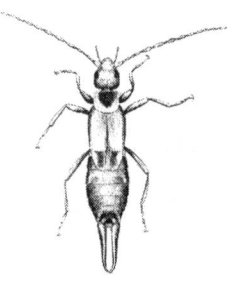
- **Earwigs** take advantage of narrow harborages found in accumulated debris around houses and outbuildings. They are good flyers and will move from there to houses. **See page 92.**

- **Rats** may not find anything to eat in accumulated trash and debris, but they can use this as a nest site and move from there to forage in garages or indoors. Inspect for burrows and entry points. **See pages 134, 135.**

- **Deer mice** may nest in these site or visit them in search of food. From these locations mice can move to the perimeter of houses or other structures. **See page 137.**

- **Raccoons** are scavengers and will often visit trash and debris sites in search of food. They may nest there for short periods. **See page 143.**

TREES, PLANTS, TURFGRASS

- **Boxelder bugs** feed on the seeds of maple trees (boxelder is a maple). The presence of boxelder or other maples trees in the neighborhood may supply food for these bugs. **See page 58.**

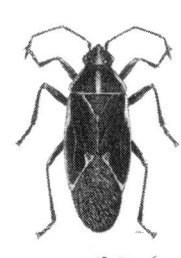

- **Elm leaf beetles** attack elm trees. The larvae eat the surface of the leaves. The adult beetles over-winter outside or inside (attics). The pale green color of these beetles makes them easy to identify. **See page 79.**

- **Tent caterpillars** attack a variety of trees, but usually prefer wild cherry. The large 'tents' are built in the spring. The caterpillars are inside the tent during the day and leave to feed on the leaves at night. **See page 110.**

- **Aphids** are pests of almost all ornamental trees, shrubs, and other plantings. They are present throughout the spring and summer. They suck plant sap and produce honeydew that ants feed on. Controlling aphids will help control ants. **See page 57.**

- **Spots on leaves** and other discolorations of leaves on ornamental plants are probably not caused by insecticides. They are most likely caused by aphids or other insects that attack plants. **See page 59.**

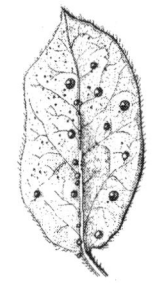

TREES, PLANTS, TURFGRASS Cont.

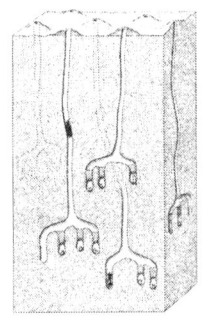

- **Sweat bees** build their nests in exposed soil, often on banks that face the sun. There may be a large number of holes and these small bees will be active during the heat of the day. They may be attracted to people working nearby. **See page 40.**

- **Cicada killer wasps** are active in late summer and fall, when the annual cicadas are singing in trees. These large wasps dig holes in exposed soil or turfgrass then capture a cicada to place in the hole. These wasps are not usually aggressive, and their activity is usually limited to a few weeks. **See page 50.**

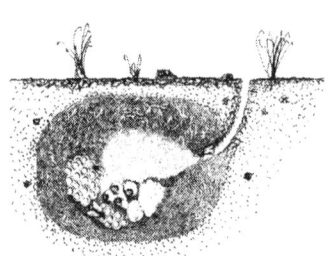

- **Bumble bees** are active in spring when the over-wintering queens look for a nest site. They often select old mouse and chipmunk burrows. Nests may be adjacent to houses and concealed among plants, and also under decks. **See page 49.**

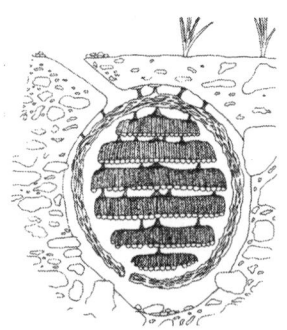

- **Yellowjackets** will build below-ground nests in protected places, such as along the edge of a flower garden, or in the open. The opening to the nest is often difficult to see. In fall these nests can have a large number of wasps. **See pages 51 - 54.**

TREES, PLANTS, TURFGRASS Cont.

- **Black Formica ants** are common around houses; they build low-profile mounds in turfgrass, usually on slopes facing the sun. These ants forage for honeydew from aphids in trees and shrubs, and they occur on flowers. They can be mistaken for carpenter ants. **See page 48.**

- **Yellow ants** are common around structures. Nests may be around the perimeter and along the foundation of buildings, and under concrete slabs. Colonies produce swarms in the spring and fall, and the winged females can be confused with termite swarmers. **See page 42.**

- **Fire ants** are now common in residential areas and their mounds can be seen along the edge of turfgrass and sometimes close to structures. **See page 47.**

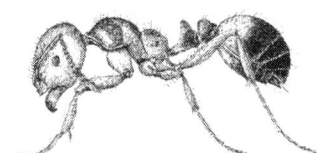

- **Ticks** are common along the edges of turfgrass, where there may be an edge with shrubs, a wooded area, or simply in areas where there is tall and uncut grass. The American dog tick and the Lone star tick are the most common in these locations. **See pages 118 - 120.**

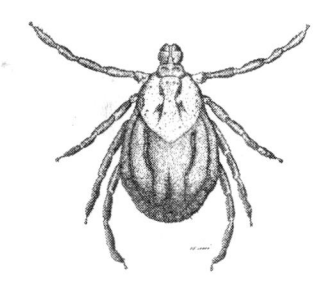

- **Deer ticks** are common in areas that have a white-tail deer populations and deer mice. The adult ticks feed on the large animals, but the nymphs feed on deer mice. This small tick spreads Lyme disease to people, dogs, and cats. **See page 120.**

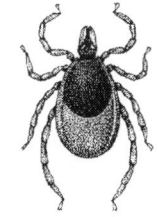

- **Millipedes** live and feed in the thatch layer of turfgrass. Sometimes conditions result in large populations developing, and when the habitat becomes crowded, large numbers of millipedes migrate. **See page 132.**

 GUIDE TO HOUSEHOLD AND WOOD INFESTING PESTS

TREES, PLANTS, TURFGRASS Cont.

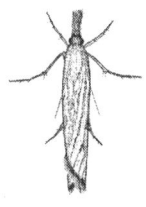

- **Sod webworm moths** are commonly seen flying across turfgrass at sunset. These moths collect at outdoor lights and sometimes come indoors. They are distinguished from meal moths by their long shape. **See page 109.**

- **Bag worms** are caterpillars that live in a protective case as they feed on the leaves of trees, especially evergreens. The cocoons may remain on the tree or be found on the sides of buildings. **See page 109.**

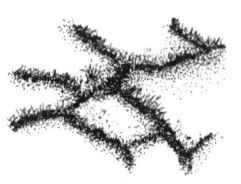 

- **Voles** are small rodents that feed on plant material in burrows below the ground. . They make extensive runways; after snow melt exposes their above-ground tunnels can be seen. **See page 138.**

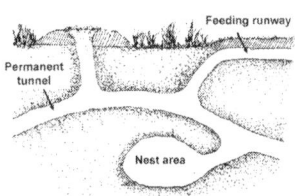 

- **Moles** are below-ground feeders on insects and earthworms. Their feeding tunnels are visible in turfgrass in the spring and fall. **See page 138.**

- **Squirrels** are a pest of turfgrass when they are searching for food and dig small holes in grass and flower beds. They are searching for nuts and bulbs that they will eat. **See pages 139, 140.**

- **Skunks** forage at night and come to the perimeter of houses and other buildings in search of food scraps. They dig small holes in turfgrass searching for grubs below the surface. The damage to turf can be extensive if there is an infestation of beetle grubs. **See page 143.**

WOOD DECK, PORCH

- **Carpenter bees** search for exposed wood to build their nest. Females select flat surfaces and end grain pieces of wood. They are active in spring; they can be distinguished from bumble bees by their shiny abdomen. **See page 40.**

- **Carpenter ants and Acrobat ants** build nests in exposed wood, especially wood that has been damaged by moisture. Carpenter ants nesting in decking wood may forage away from the site. Carpenter ants forage at night late in summer. Acrobat ant nests are small and may be noticed by the powdery frass that falls from openings in the galleries. **See pages 43, 44.**

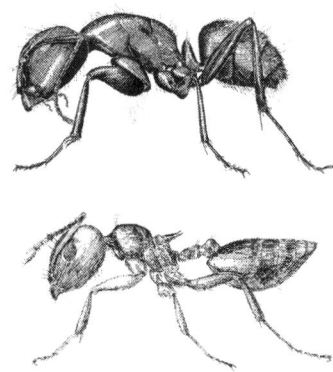

- **Skunks** are active at night and are unnoticed except for the odor they leave behind. In spring females may nest in protected sites under ground-level decks and porches. Sealing access to these areas will prevent this behavior. **See page 143.**

- **Bumble bees** often build nests at the edge or under ground-level decks and porches; they select old mouse burrows as a nest site. Unless they are threatening people, the nests may simply be left alone. **See page 49.**

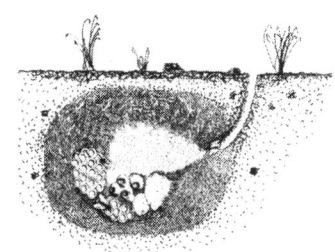

 GUIDE TO HOUSEHOLD AND WOOD INFESTING PESTS

AROUND FOUNDATION

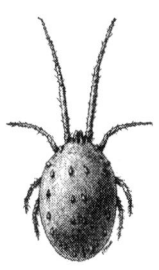

- **Clover mites** are common problems in spring. Large populations in turfgrass cause mites to move onto foundation walls and then up to windows and inside houses. These mites are common in newly established turfgrass. **See page 120.**

- **Yellow ants** are common around foundations; they build their nests in the soil close to the foundation wall. Colonies produce swarmers (winged ants) in spring and fall, and they are sometimes confused with termite swarmers. **See page 42.**

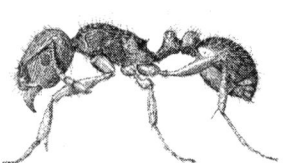

- **Pavement ants** are common around house. They build their nests in the soil close to the foundation, and sometimes establish a nest between the sill plate and the top of the foundation wall. **See page 42.**

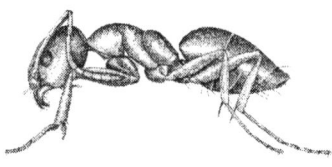

- **Odorous house ants** commonly build nests around the foundation of houses; they forage indoors and outdoors (aphids). They may move the nest permanently indoors. **See page 47.**

- **Chipmunks** build ground nests along foundation walls and adjacent shrubs. They forage for food along the foundation, in garbage containers, and out into the surrounding turf. **See page 139.**

- **Deer mice** are common around foundations in fall when temperatures drop and the foundation retains heat over-night. Once close to the foundation they will look for entry point into the house or other building. **See page 137.**

AROUND FOUNDATION Cont.

- **Mason bees** are often seen around foundations and brick veneer on buildings. In spring females look for small holes to enlarge and use for a nest site. They will tunnel into old mortar between bricks to build a singular nest. **See page 49.**

- **Wolf spiders** are common on the ground around foundations; here they hunt for insects and other prey. They can move indoors through cracks and crevices around doors and windows. **See page 128.**

- **Black widow spiders** can be found along the foundation, especially near the openings to crawl spaces, near crawl space vents, and near downspouts. **See page 130.**

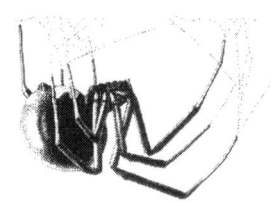

- **Field crickets** are often seen around foundations in fall when nighttime temperatures are low. The foundation retains warmth into the night and these crickets come to the heat source, then they move indoors. They do not survive indoors because it is too dry for them. **See page 91.**

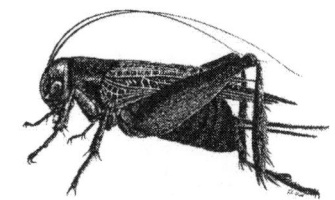

- **Sowbugs** are common in the mulch and decaying organic matter around foundations. They move inside when their habitat become too wet or too dry. They die indoors because of the low humidity. **See page 122.**

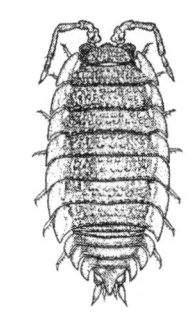

 GUIDE TO HOUSEHOLD AND WOOD INFESTING PESTS

MODERN LOG HOUSE

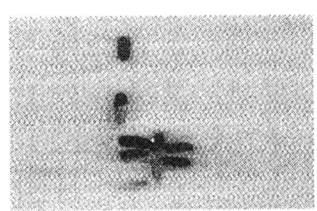

- **Ambrosia beetle** galleries are easily recognized by the dark blue or black staining. These beetles were active when the log was freshly cut and the wood moisture was high. They do not remain active in seasoned wood. **See page 70.**

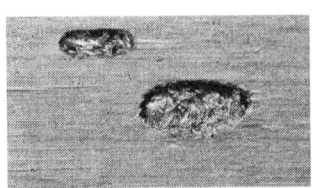

- **Pine sawyer** galleries are recognized by the presence of fibrous frass and the oval shape. These beetles infest the live tree or when it was freshly cut, they do not re-infest seasoned wood. **See page 67.**

- **Buprestid beetle or flat-headed borer** galleries are distinguished by their flattened oval shape. These beetles may be in standing timber or when it is freshly cut. They sometimes occur in seasoned logs, but only rarely re-infest. They do not cause structural damage. **See page 70.**

- **Solitary bees** sometimes use the galleries of wood-infesting beetles as a nest site. They may excavate the gallery and remove old frass or produce some new frass when they chew into the wood. This can give the false impression of an active beetle infestation.

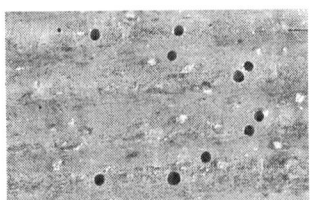

- **Anobiid beetle** exit holes can be found in some logs used for modern log houses. Typically the infestation is not active, but there may be some frass falling from the holes. **See pages 64, 65.**

MODERN LOG HOUSE Cont.

- **Carpenter bees** are attracted to exposed wood, especially the end grain of some logs. They often return to the same location year after year and infestations can damage logs. **See page 40.**

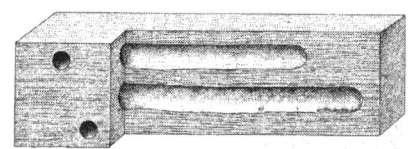

- **Carpenter ants** are a major pest of log houses, especially when rainwater is not kept off the sides and away from the corners where logs meet. These ants will find and build nests in moisture-damaged wood. **See page 43.**

- **Acrobat ants** take advantage of moisture-damaged wood on porches and decks and establish nests. They may be unnoticed until the powdery frass from their galleries is seen. **See page 44.**

- **Woodpeckers** are attracted to the sides of log houses for several reasons, one may be the presence of insect below the wood surface. The nests of carpenter bees contain many larvae that these birds can detect. **See page 144.**

SWIMMING POOLS

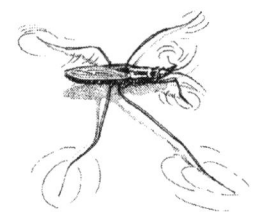

- **Water striders** often occur on the surface of swimming pools in suburban areas. They can walk on the surface of water because of non-wettable hairs on their feet. The adults can fly long distances from natural ponds to pools. They will not infest swimming pools. **See page 60.**

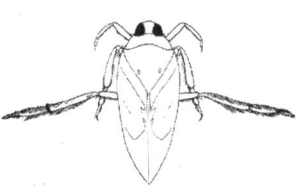

- **Back swimmers** fly to swimming pools from nearby ponds and lakes; they are attracted to light at night. They swim underwater with a long sweeping stroke of their back legs. These insects are known to bite people in swimming pools. **See page 60.**

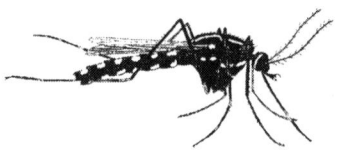

- **Mosquitoes** will not live in swimming pools, but they may occur around pools and rest in the vegetation around swimming pools. Mosquito larvae do not survive in swimming pools. **See pages 103, 104.**

CHAPTER 3
ANTS, BEES, WASPS

Ants, bees, and wasps have a range of habits: some are solitary, some live in large colonies, some are plant feeders, and some are parasites or predators. They have chewing mouthparts, and they use their mandibles to chew wood and build 'paper' nests. Some species, such as bees, can lap water and nectar from flowers.

Ants, bees, and wasps build a nest that contains the colony. The colony survives by dividing the labor of building and maintaining the nest. Queens start the colony and lay eggs, workers, which are sterile females, gather food, maintain and repair, and defend the colony.

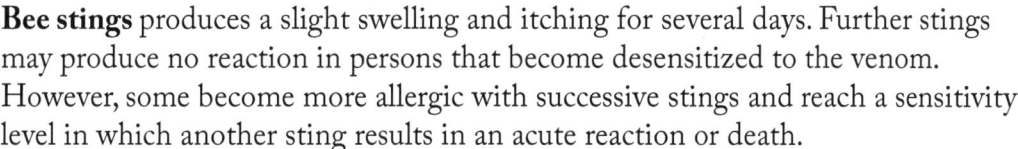

Ant colonies usually start when males and females fly from the nest and mate. After mating, females form a nest by making a brood chamber and begin laying eggs. Workers of the first brood forage and feed the queen, and expand the nest. The founding queen continues to lay eggs and remains in the nest. When the colony reaches a certain size the queen lays eggs that develop into reproductive females and males, and the process starts again.

Bee stings produces a slight swelling and itching for several days. Further stings may produce no reaction in persons that become desensitized to the venom. However, some become more allergic with successive stings and reach a sensitivity level in which another sting results in an acute reaction or death.

Nests of bees and wasps are often built in the soil at the perimeter of structures or in turfgrass. Sweat bees are commonly seen in spring as they build nests in exposed soil. Cicada killer wasps are active in fall when they are excavating holes in the ground to hold the cicadas they have captured.

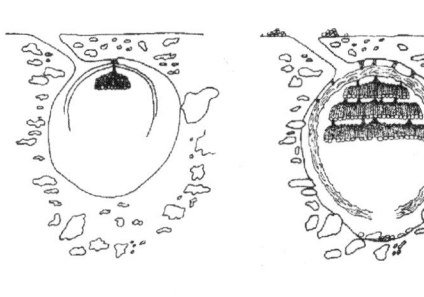

Yellowjackets build a nest in the ground as large as the familiar nests in trees and shrubs. Below-ground nests start with a single queen excavating an abandoned mouse burrow. Once the first and second brood of workers develop the nets expands with more and more brood cells. By late summer the nest may have several thousand workers.

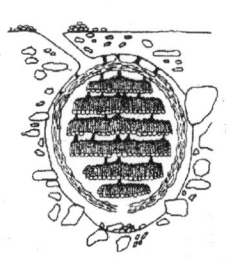

Carpenter Bees

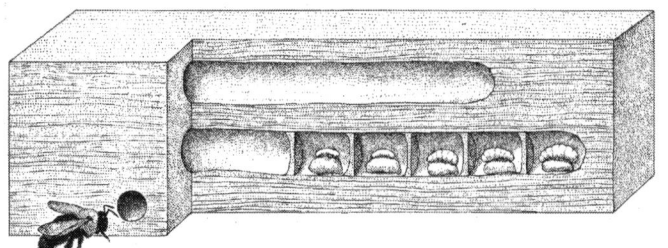

These are large black and yellow bees that look like bumble bees. The abdomen of carpenter bees is shiny, but it is covered with fine hair in bumble bees.

Nests are built in exposed wood, including house siding, and decking. Adults over-winter in the nest or in protected locations outdoors. Mating occurs in spring. Females may use an old gallery, create a new gallery, or make a new one from an entrance used by other females.

Colony. Females make a 1/2 inch diameter hole. After excavating the long gallery, they begin preparing individual cells. Pollen and nectar are placed together and the female deposits an egg on it. Over several days she will create about 6 cells in the gallery. Larval development is complete in about 2 weeksw, and adults appear in about 1 month. The first bee to become an adult is usually in the cell at the end of the gallery. The adult cuts through the partitions of all the cells to emerge.

Sweat Bees

These small bees have a black body; the thorax and abdomen have yellowish-white setae.

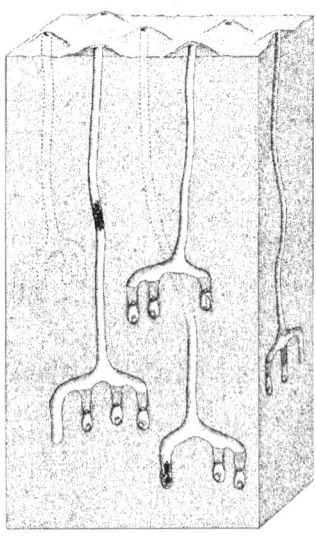

Nests are usually made in clay soil, many nests may occur together. Females excavate a long burrow in the ground; along the sides of the burrow are short branches that lead to a brood cell. These cells contain pollen and nectar and a single egg. Several females may use one burrow.

Habits. They are attracted to perspiring (sweating) individuals. Although they are non-threatening, they will sting when there is activity near the nest.

Ants

Ants are the most abundant insects on earth. Although there are thousands of species, relatively few ants are indoor or outdoor pests. Most of these have specific habits or infestation sites: carpenter ants build nests in structural wood; Pharaoh ants and thief ants live almost exclusively indoors; Odorous house ants nest outdoors but forage indoors. Fire ants usually nest outdoors in large colonies.

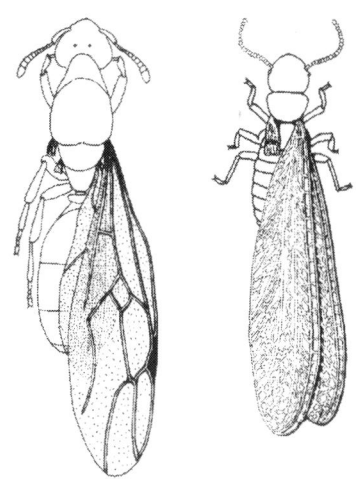

Ant colonies produce winged adults at least once a year, usually in spring and summer. Large numbers of males and females fly from the nest and collect on the outside of buildings. Some swarms occur indoors. Subterranean termites have the same swarming schedule. Termites usually swarm on warm days in spring followinbg a rain.

Winged Ant   Winged Termite

- Swarming ants are sometimes mistaken for termites because they are about the same size and color.

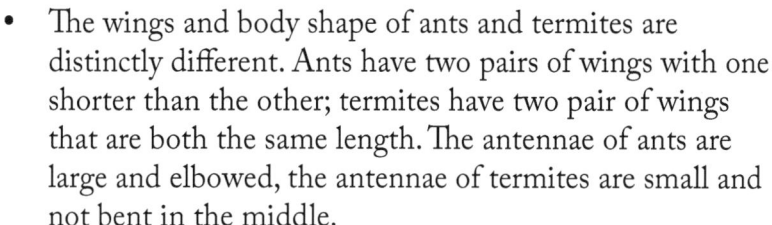

- The wings and body shape of ants and termites are distinctly different. Ants have two pairs of wings with one shorter than the other; termites have two pair of wings that are both the same length. The antennae of ants are large and elbowed, the antennae of termites are small and not bent in the middle.

Crazy Ant

Worker body color is dark brown to blackish brown. Body is very slender and the legs are extremely long.

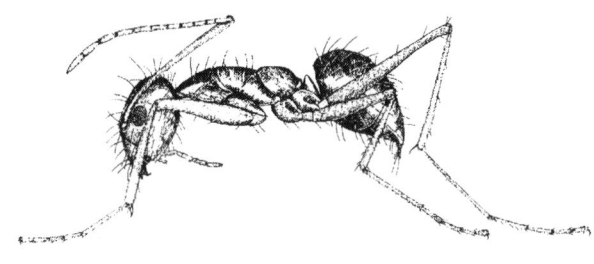

Nests indoors are often in wall voids. Outdoor nets are around buildings and sites such as trash cans and refuse dumpsters. They occur on the ground- and upper-floors of commercial buildings. The long legs of these ants make their walking seem unorganized, which is the origin of their name, crazy ants.

Larger Yellow Ant

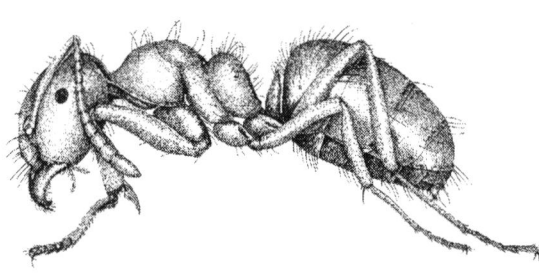

Worker body color ranges from uniform yellowish brown to dark brown. The swarming adults have the same body color, and their wings are light brown.

Nests are in exposed soil or under stones or logs. In open areas the nests are sometimes in small mounds. Nests may be around the perimeter and along the foundation of buildings, and under concrete slabs.

Colony. Nest construction and foraging is done primarily at night. <u>Outdoors</u>, winged males and females emerge from mid-March to July, but some swarms can occur as late as September. <u>Indoors</u>, swarming may occur from late fall to early spring. This ant is often confused with the swarms of subterranean termites, because of light brown color and spring and fall swarming habits.

Pavement Ant

Worker body color ranges from light brown to blackish brown; the legs are light brown. The surface of the head and thorax has distinct longitudinal grooves.

Nests are in exposed soil or under stones, pavement, and along sidewalks. Indoor nests may be in masonry walls and along the foundation.

Colony. These ants have large colonies with one functional queen. Winged males and females swarm in June and July, but they may emerge almost any time of the year.

Habits. Natural food includes live and dead insects, honeydew, plant sap, and seeds. Indoors they forage for meat and grease. Nests are sometimes positioned between the wood sill and the top of the foundation wall. Refuse expelled from the nest site includes fragments of seeds, dead insects, and fine wood fibers. The presence of wood fibers can be alarming, but these ants do not infest wood.

Western Black Carpenter Ant

Worker body color is black and there are strong hairs on the body. The legs are usually dark red.

Nests are established in damp or decaying wood. Mature colonies contain 9,000-50,000 workers.

Colony. Egg laying is from April to June. Larval development is during summer, most of the workers are produced by October. Egg production stops by August and September, and the larvae present in the colony over-winter with the queen. No food is consumed by the colony from October through January.

Habits. This is the dominant carpenter ant in northwestern U.S. and adjacent areas in Canada. The satellite colonies can be large, and from these they can move into and infest a nearby structure. Damage to structural wood can occur in a short time and is not limited to moisture damaged wood. Satellite colonies in houses can contain several thousand ants.
These ants create trails between the main colony and the satellites.

Eastern Black Carpenter Ant

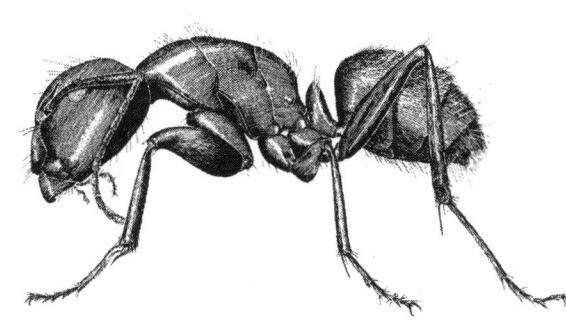

Worker body color is typically black; some may be reddish black. The large size of the queen and workers of this ant is makes it easy to identify.

Nests are in dead trees, and in rotting logs and stumps. Indoor nests are in moisture-damaged wood and also sound wood.

Colony. Activity begins in April and extends to November. In some regions. They are inactive from December to April. Colonies 3-5 years old produce swarms.

Habits. Foraging peaks soon after sunset and extends into the night, and peaks again before sunrise. The connection between satellite nests and the main colony nest site is through well established trails.

 GUIDE TO HOUSEHOLD AND WOOD INFESTING PESTS

Acrobat Ants

Workers are yellowish brown to blackish brown. These small ants are identified by their heart-shaped abdomen

Nests indoors are in structural wood exposed to moisture, such as roofing, siding, and porches, and also door and window frames.

Colonies. Acrobat ant colonies are usually small and contain 2,000-3,000 workers. Winged males and females emerge from early June to November.

Habits. The common name, acrobat ant, is derived from their habit of raising their abdomen over the head and thorax when disturbed. Workers will bite and give off an odor when alarmed. Infestations may be discovered by the powdery frass that falls from the nest galleries. These ants will make trails from their foraging sites outdoors to the nest site in wood. Enclosed decks and porches with wood frames are often infested.

Argentine Ant

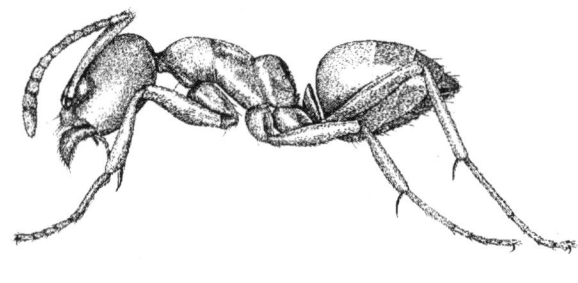

Workers are light brown or brown.

Nests indoors are in refuse piles, bird nests, in wall voids, masonry voids, and in cracks in concrete slabs around the perimeter of buildings. Nests may be deep in the ground during dry or cold weather.

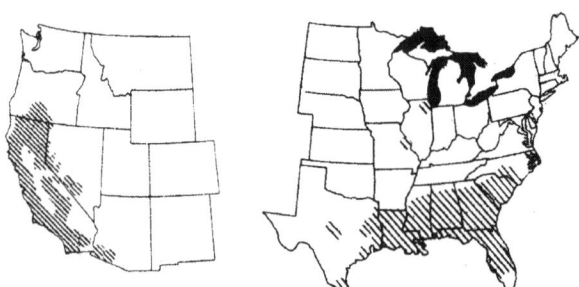

Colony. The colonies of these ants are large and contain hundreds of queens. New colonies are formed when a queen and a small number of workers migrate to a new site. In winter, several colonies may combine to form a large colony.

Habits. Argentine ants produce a chemical trail, which allows them to forage day and night. Food includes sweets, meats, fruit, eggs, dairy products, animal fats and vegetable oils. Excessively dry or wet conditions often cause workers to invade houses. Colonies can become dominant in an area and effectively force out other ant species, such as Odorous house ants.

Pharaoh Ant

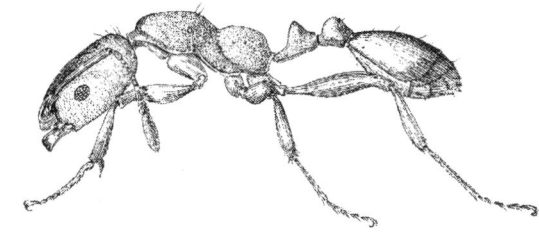

Workers are yellowish brown to reddish brown. The segments of antennal club gradually increase in size to the end.

Nests indoors are in small secluded locations, such as in light switches, behind baseboards, and in cabinets. The nest sites are small and are frequently moved.

Colony. These ants are active all year and colonies can be large. New colonies are formed when a young queen and a small number of workers split from the parent colony.

Habits. Workers forage 24 hours per day and use chemical trails. Indoor they feed on sweets, meat, grease, and a variety of other materials.

Thief Ant

Worker body is shiny; yellowish brown to dark brown. Last segment (only) of the antenna is large and elongate.

Nests are in wood, masonry, and household materials. The nets are usually in secluded voids.

Colony. Swarms occur from July to October. Colonies contain several hundred to several thousand individuals. Winged forms emerge from July to October.

Habits. Food indoors includes meat, sweets, ripened fruit, oils, and dairy products. They prefer food with high protein content.

Little Black Ant

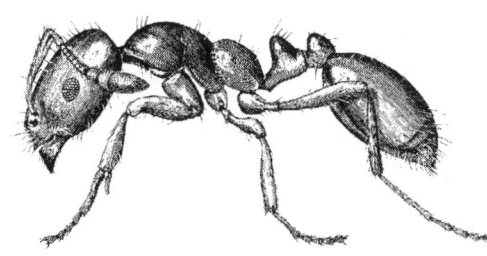

Worker body is shiny, dark brown to black. Antennae have a 3-segmented club.

Nests indoors are in structural wood or in the masonry of the foundation. Winged forms emerge from June to August.

Habits. Food indoors includes meats, sweets, bread, grease, oils, cereals, and fruit juices.

GUIDE TO HOUSEHOLD AND WOOD INFESTING PESTS

Ghost Ant

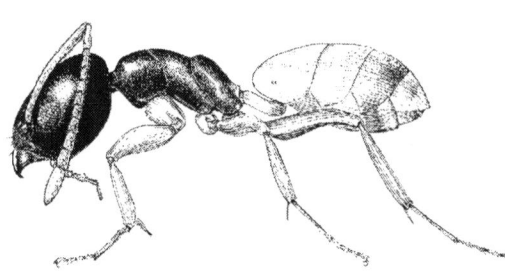

Head and thorax brown, abdomen is yellowish brown; antennae and legs are pale brown.

Nests indoors are in voids and cavities, such as in closets and in discarded clothing.

Colony. Colonies contain several hundred workers and several females. Food is primarily sweets. Nests in southern regions are outdoors, in northern regions nests are indoors. They have been found infesting buildings much like Pharaoh ants.

White-footed Ant

Worker body is blackish brown to black, and the tarsi are pale yellow.

Nests indoors are in wall voids, potted plants, and household materials; there may be several satellite nests. Trails are made outside buildings, indoors the tails are along the edges of baseboards
and carpeting.

Colony. Winged females emerge in May and June. Indoors they feed on sweets.

Red Imported Fire Ant

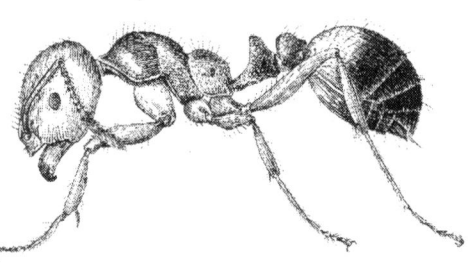

Workers are yellowish brown to blackish brown.

Nests are above ground mounds. Workers enter and exit through holes 6-10 feet from the mound.

Colony. Swarms occur from April to November, colonies produce 4,000-6,000 winged adults. Food includes meat, grease, and other protein-rich food.

Habits. When colonies are disturbed workers become aggressive and deliver a painful sting.

Southern Fire Ant

Workers have a reddish yellow head and thorax, and the abdomen dark brown.

Nests are irregular mounds in loose soil, or under stones and sometimes in the masonry of houses. Nests can cover an area of several square feet.

Colony. Swarms occur from April to October, colonies are usually large. Food includes meat, grease, and nuts.

Habits. This native fire ant will become aggressive and sting when the nest is disturbed.

Odorous House Ant

Body color is uniform brown to black. Workers are less than 1/8 inch long. They are sometimes difficult to distinguish from Argentine ants, but the Odorous house ant has the smell of coconut when crushed.

Nests indoors are numerous and scattered throughout the house. Nests are usually associated with moisture, such as in wall voids near water pipes, and in termite-damaged wood. A typical outdoor nest consists of a main colony and several satellite colonies, each with a queen and brood.

Colony. Each colony may have 200 functional queens; swarmers are produced in colonies that are 4-5 years old. Workers establish trails leading from the nest to the food, and follow along tree limbs, the edges of buildings, baseboards, and kitchen counter tops.

Habits. When a nest is disturbed, workers run rapidly, emitting an odor from their elevated abdomens. These ants can bite. <u>Outdoors</u>, they feed on honeydew from aphids located close to the structure. <u>Indoors</u>, are usually found near a moisture source, such as wall voids, behind paneling and behind baseboards, near water heaters, and along wall-to-wall carpeting. The satellite nests indoors are small and may be moved frequently.

GUIDE TO HOUSEHOLD AND WOOD INFESTING PESTS

Mound Ants

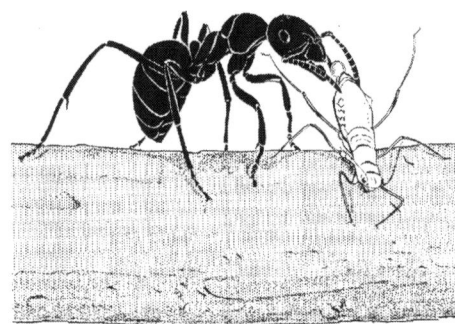

Formica species ants build a nest mound that may extend only slightly above the surface of the soil, or one that is well above the surface, as in the Allegheny mound ant. These are relatively large ants that forage during the day on plants and trees; they feed on insects and take honeydew from aphids.

Allegheny Mound Ant

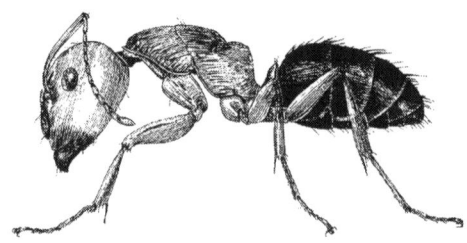

The head and thorax are reddish-orange, the abdomen and legs are brownish black.

Nests are large mounds in wooded areas or in suburban turfgrass. Several mounds may be connected by tunnels that may extend into the ground and upwards in the mound.

Vegetation, including small trees and shrubs, is killed within 50 feet of their mounds.

Colony. Allegheny mound ant colonies have multiple queens.

Habits. When a nest is disturbed the workers swarm out in large numbers and will aggressively bite.

Black Formica Ant

The body and legs are black, the surface is not shiny.

Nests are small mounds in the soil in open areas. Workers forage on trees and shrubs close and far from the nest.

Colony. This species typically has a single queen.

Habits. Workers will swarm out of a disturbed nest, but they are generally not aggressive. They are common in spring as soon as flowers emerge and aphids become active. Workers are common on spring flowers, especially peonies. They are often misidentified as carpenter ants, but they are generally smaller than carpenter ants.

Mud Daubers

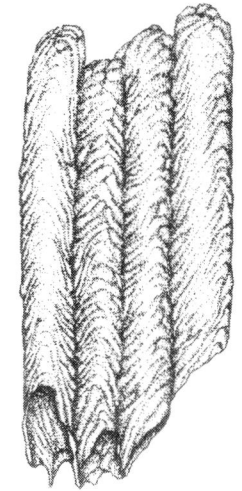

Body is shiny black, dark blue, or with black and yellow markings.

Nest cells are provisioned with spiders. After the female constructs the chambers she captures spiders to place in the cells as a larval food. An egg is laid in each cell and it is sealed.

Habits. These wasps build mud cells in parallel rows, some species build small rounded nests made of mud. These wasp capture spiders for their nests, including black widow spiders.

Mason Bees

Body is metallic blue or green; these are small bees with a fuzzy body.

Nests are small earthen cells in brick veneer of houses. Nests may be in beetle exit holes in wood, or in soil. Females burrow into the soft mortar of stone- and brickwork, and line their nest cells with soil.

Habits. These bees have strong mandibles and can tunnel into old or soft mortar. When they excavate exit holes of wood-infesting beetles, frass is scattered and may give the impression of beetle activity.

Bumble Bees

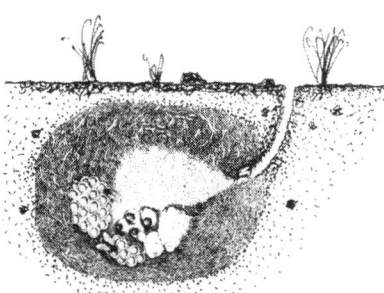

Body is covered with setae, usually black with yellow bands.

Nests are usually in old mouse burrow in soil. Colonies last one season, at end of summer colonies contain about 100 workers.

Habits. Nests are often built close to buildings and in soil around ornamental shrubs.

Cicada Killer Wasp

These are large wasps. The body is dark brown with reddish orange legs, and yellow markings on the thorax and abdomen. There are several species of cicada killer wasps, one species occurs east of the Rocky Mountains, two species occur in western U.S., and two species in Florida.

Nests are burrows in the soil. Nesting occurs in late summer and fall, at the time that annual cicadas emerge and begin singing in trees. The prey is cicadas captured in trees.

Habits. The female flies around the tree or shrub in a circular pattern. When a cicada is located, it is stung and the wasp grasps it and flies back to the burrow. Female may dig burrows that contain 15 cells provisioned with 1-3 cicadas each. Females are generally not aggressive, but males will protect areas around burrows.

Umbrella Wasps

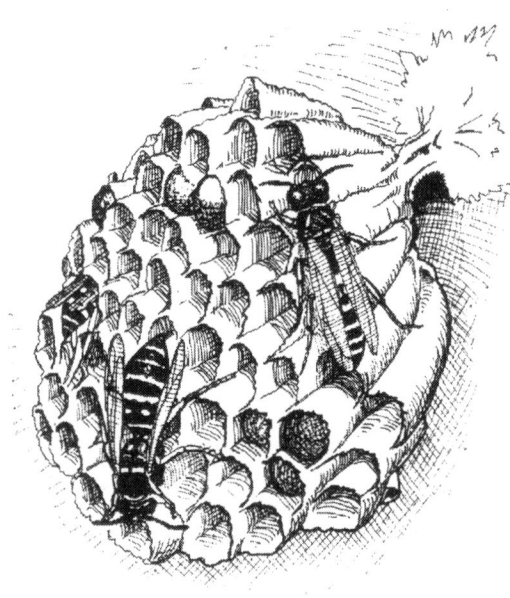

Workers are brown to blackish brown, and with yellow marking on the abdomen.

Nests are initiated in spring by one or more queens. Cloudy and rainy weather in spring will limit the number of new nests formed, and queens may share a nest. These nests develop quickly and are often large.

Habits. Nests are used one season and queens over-winter. A new nest is often built next to the queen's original nest, and the result may be a large number of new and used nests in one site. They prey on caterpillars and also feed on honeydew, and bruised fruits. Queens from nests along house soffits will often over-winter indoors and become active in late fall and spring.

European Hornet

Body is brownish black body and with narrow to broad yellow bands on the abdomen.

Nests are usually built in trees, attics, and walls of houses. A brown envelope and large cells distinguish this species from large yellowjackets. A mature nest has about 1,000 workers. Nests often have a foul odor, and when they are built in an attic the nest can extend to the living space.

Habits. Prey includes grasshoppers, cicadas, flies, yellowjackets, and honey bees. Workers fly and hunt for prey at night, and they are attracted to outdoor lights, and lighted windows. These are very large hornets and their behavior of hunting at night and coming to lights can be threatening.

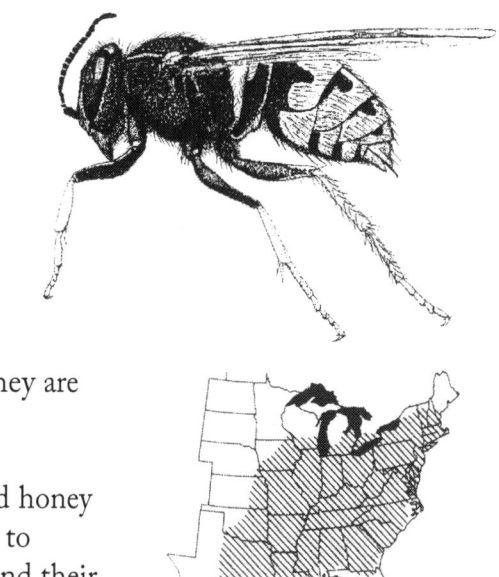

Baldfaced Hornet (Yellowjacket)

Workers are black with white markings. The dorsal surface of abdominal segments 1-3 is entirely black.

Nests are usually established in ornamental bushes and trees, electric power poles, houses, sheds, and other structures. Colonies decline in September.
The majority of nests contain less than 2,000 cells.

Habits. Workers forage flies and other yellowjackets.

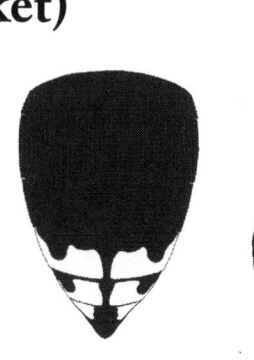 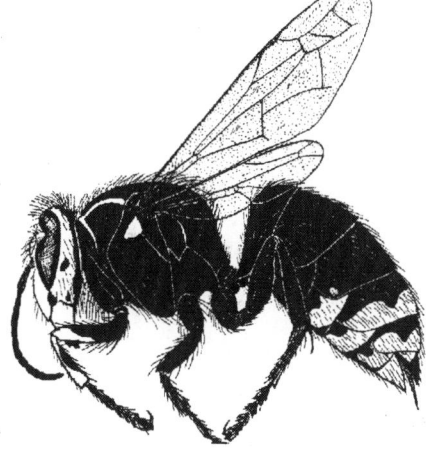

GUIDE TO HOUSEHOLD AND WOOD INFESTING PESTS

Aerial Yellowjacket

Body is black with yellow markings. The yellow bands on abdomen segments are distinct.

Nests may be in shrubs or bushes, and in the tops of trees, and in structures. Mature nest can have from 644 to 4,290 cells, and there may be as many as 7 combs.

Habits. The large paper nests of this species are usually built well above the ground and away from the reach of potential predators. Workers forage during the day for grasshoppers, tree crickets, caterpillars, flies, and spiders. They are attracted to sugar in late summer. By late summer there are no larvae in the nest and workers are not foraging for protein to feed young and at this time they prefer carbohydrates as an energy food.

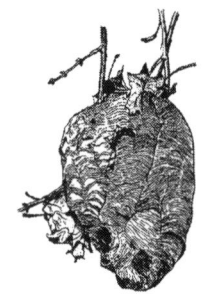

German Yellowjacket

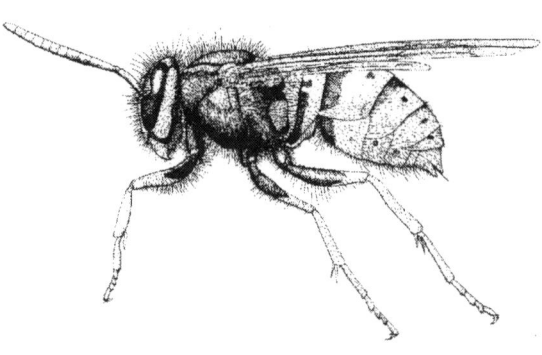

Body is brown with yellow marking on head, thorax, and bands on the abdomen. The marking on the abdomen are distinct for this species.

Nests may contain as many as 2,000 workers. They are often built in attics and wall cavities. Colonies are usually last for 1 year.

Habits. This species preys on a variety of arthropods. Most workers forage close to the nest site.

Common Yellowjacket

Abdomen has distinct yellow bands, the first segment of the antenna is entirely black. The thorax lacks the two stripes that are characteristic of the Southern yellowjacket.

Nests are usually built in decaying logs or stumps. The nest envelope is made of rotten wood fiber and is brittle. Nest size can be nearly 3,000. Colonies are started in May or June, the peak activity is in September And some are active until October.

Habits. Prey includes caterpillars, flies, and other flying insects. As the name indicates, this is one of the most common species.

Western Yellowjacket

Body is and black and yellow. Antennal segment 1 is yellow at the end.

Nests are usually built in subterranean cavities, but occasionally in walls of buildings. Nests may contain nearly 4,000 workers when the colony it at a peak.

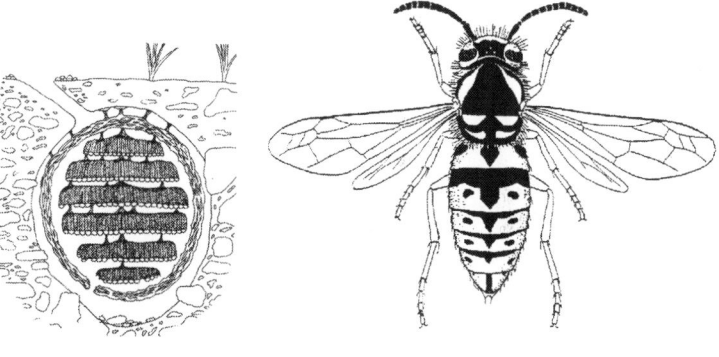

Habits. The workers prey on spiders, grasshoppers, and flies. Periodic outbreaks occur every 3-5 years. Cloudy and wet weather in spring limits the food available for founding queens, and the number of successful nests decreases. Following a relatively warm and dry spring there may be an increase in the number of successful colonies, and in late summer and fall the workers can be a nuisance around buildings and recreation areas.

Eastern Yellowjacket

There is an anchor-shaped black mark on abdomen segment 1. The first antennal segment is black.

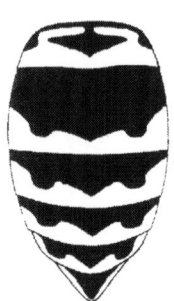

Nests are usually subterranean. In urban environments, nests are in the walls of houses and other buildings. Colonies usually have peak numbers of workers in August or September. Nests contain 2,000-5,000 workers.

Habits. This species often builds nests underground around the perimeter of houses and commercial buildings. The opening to the underground nest may be hidden. The nest is often in a shaded location or protected from rainfall. In these sites the nest may be disturbed accidentally and the wasps become aggressive. Colonies contain a large number of workers in fall and they will remain active until the first or second frost.

Southern Yellowjacket

Body has yellow and black markings; the abdomen has narrow yellow bands. The thorax has two distinct parallel stripes.

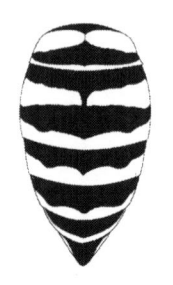

Nests are located in turfgrass surrounding houses and buildings, recreation areas, and roadsides. Colonies contain 500-4,000 workers.

Habits. This yellowjacket is a social parasite of other yellowjacket species. The parasite queen takes over the nest from the host queen and assumes complete control of the colony. This species will vigorously defend its nest. In fall there are many workers are in the colony.

CHAPTER 4

BED BUGS, STINK BUGS, BOXELDER BUGS

Bed bugs are blood-sucking parasites of humans and other animals. The nymph and adults require blood to develop and survive. They live in cracks and crevices near their host, and travel at night to get a blood meal. These small insects can detect the heat and carbon dioxide given off by animals. Bed bugs depend on humans to survive and spread, there are no natural populations of this insect. They are spread in luggage, bedroom furniture, and bed frames. Adults can survive long periods without feeding and live 9-12 months.

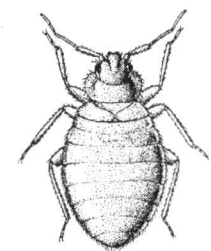

- Although all stages of bed bugs suck blood of humans, these insects do not spread any diseases. They are primarily a nuisance pest.

Stink bugs suck the sap from ornamental plants and agricultural crops. The Brown marmorated stink bug is recognized by pale bands on the antennae and abdomen. They develop from eggs to adult during summer. Adults are formed in fall and at that time they look for a protected place to spend the winter. They gather in large numbers on the sides of building, and then move indoors around doors and windows.

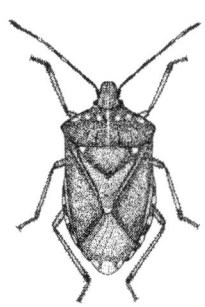

- These bugs often rest in harborages in kitchens and bathrooms during winter because these locations have high humidity. They become active in spring and move to windows and lights.

Boxelder bugs are red and black with red lines on the back. The immature stages have red abdomens. They suck the sap of leaves and seeds of maple and boxelder trees. Adults and nymphs are found on the trees that have the seed pods. In fall the adults gather in large aggregations on the sunny side of houses. They may move inside through cracks and crevices around windows and doors.

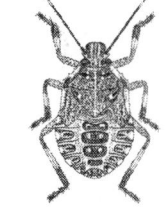

- Removing boxelder trees is not an effective method for eliminating these bugs. Boxelder bugs can feed on a variety of maple trees (boxelder is a maple).

Kudzu bugs are closely related to the brown stink bug, they have similar feeding and over-wintering habits. These bugs suck the sap of the kudzu plant, which grows as a vine in many regions of southeastern U.S. However, they can feed on other plants. When adults search for an over-wintering site they often come to the perimeter and sides of houses and large buildings.

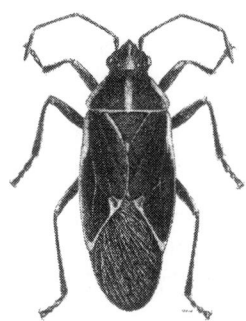

 GUIDE TO HOUSEHOLD AND WOOD INFESTING PESTS

Bed Bug

Adults are oval and somewhat flattened. Wings are absent, but there are small wingpads. The body is dark brown to reddish brown. Nymphs are similar to the adults.

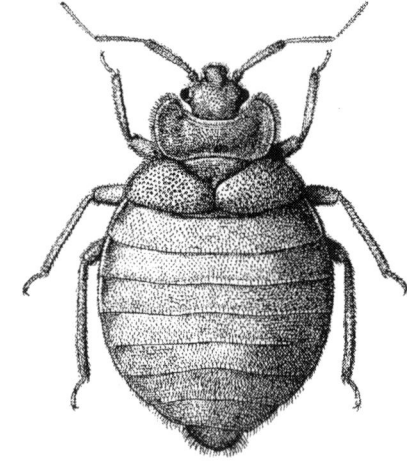

Eggs are yellowish white, and with a distinct cap at one end. Females deposit eggs in batches of 10-50; they can lay about 350. Hatching is in 6-17 days. Development to adult is through 5 nymph instars, and takes about 14 days.

Development is not completed at temperatures below 55°F. Adult males can live for about 9 months without feeding. There are 3 or 4 generations per year.

Food (blood) is required between each molt, and before egg development. Nymphs feed about every 6 days. Feeding occurs during the night and usually peaks soon after sunset and before dawn, but they will feed during the day.

Control. The majority of bed bugs in an infested room are associated with the bed, including the frame (metal or wood), the box spring, and the area immediate surrounding the bed, including furniture.

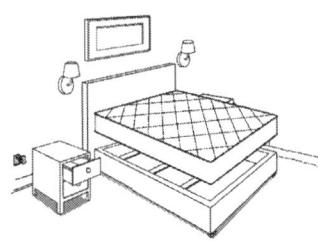

- Treat the bed frame with insecticide, and treat all cracks and crevices that are in the headboard.

- Treat underside of the box spring; remove the cover and treat the interior frame of the box spring. Discard the box spring if it is heavily infested.

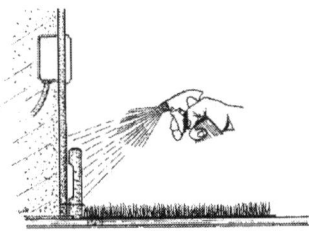

- Pictures on the wall above or close to the bed should be removed and inspected for bed bugs. Treat the back side of pictures and the edges of the picture frame.

- Treat the underside of chairs, couches and other upholstered furniture in the room.

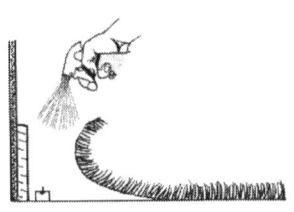

- Treat the baseboard in the areas close to the bed, and treat any furniture that is close to the bed. Apply liquid insecticide to the outside of the baseboard and apply dust behind the baseboard.

- Treat the tacking strip along the edge of the wall in rooms that have wall-to-wall carpets.

Brown Marmorated Stink Bug

Adult body color is an irregular pattern (marmorated) of dark and pale brown. Nymphs are grayish black and with a white spot on the apical third of the antenna.

Eggs are barrel-shaped, yellowish-red and deposited on the underside of leaves in batches of about 25 eggs. Hatching occurs in about 5 days. Egg-laying begins in June and continues to September. Females can produce about 400 eggs in their life time. There are five nymph stages.

Food includes seed and fruit bearing plants. Stink bugs have piercing-sucking mouthparts and suck the sap from plants.
Habits. Adults over-winter in large numbers inside and outside of buildings. Over-wintering flights of adults to new or previously infested sites begins in October and lasts for about 3 weeks. Movement to over-wintering sites begins during the day when the temperature reaches about 77° F.

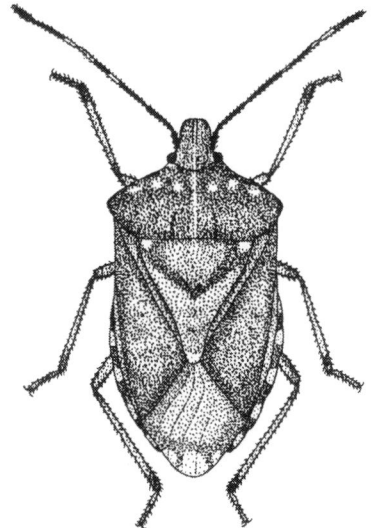

Aphids

These are soft-bodied insects that are green brown, black, and sometimes pale yellow to white. They have piercing-sucking mouthparts and can pierce the surface of plants and almost continuously suck plant sap.

Most aphids produce droplets of honeydew as they feed. Ants use this honeydew droplet as food. Honeydew is a food for many species of ants that are indoor pests, including pavement ants, carpenter ants, Odorous house ants, Ghost ants, and White-footed ants.

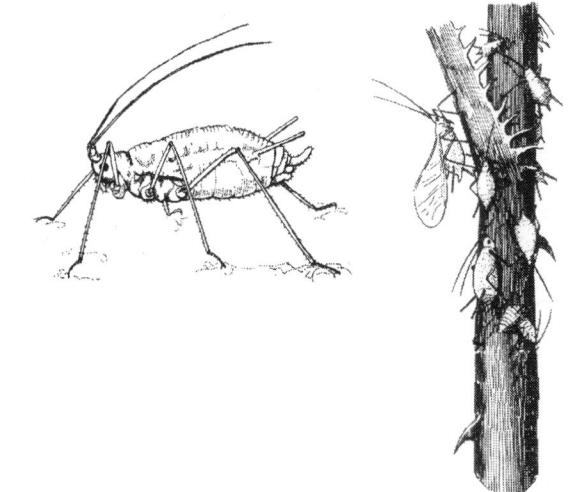

Boxelder Bug

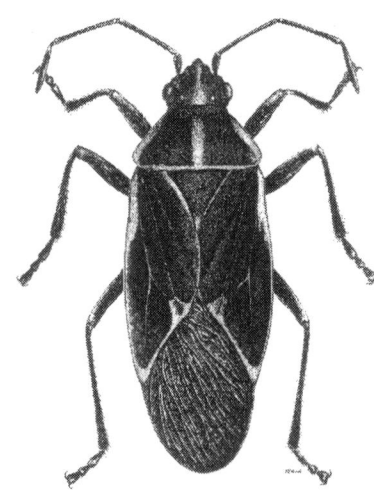

Adult body is gray-brown to black with 3 red lines on the back. The abdomen is usually red. The small nymphs are bright red and become marked with black when about half grown.

Eggs are laid on the bark and leaves of the tree; total egg per female is 200-300. Hatching occurs in about 2 weeks. Development from egg to adult takes about 2 months and there can be 3 generations per year. Adults and large nymphs of the last generation seek an over-wintering site in late fall.

Food includes the seeds, leaves, and twigs of boxelder and other maples, including silver maple, sycamore maple, and ash. It will also feed on young fruits such as apple, pear, peach, plum, and grape. Adults of the first generation feed on fallen boxelder seeds on the ground or on low vegetation. They feed on female boxelder and other maple trees once the seeds begin to form.

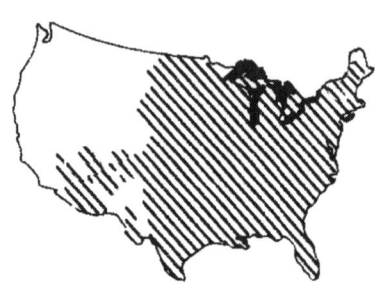

Habits. Over-wintering occurs in large numbers around house foundations and ground-floor windows. They gather on the south and west sides of buildings where the sun heats exposed surfaces; they are sensitive to small temperature differences and select the warmest substrate. Adults are capable of flying about 2 miles to find a suitable over-wintering site.

Winter harborage. Over-wintering sites selected by the Boxelder bug, Kudzu bug, and the Marmorated stink bug are usually on east or west facing walls of buildings. The sun heats the east and west sides of buildings. These sides of the houses for a long period during the day will provide the greatest warmth in winter, and will quickly warm-up in spring. The south side of buildings is cooler than the east and west sides.

Kudzu Bug

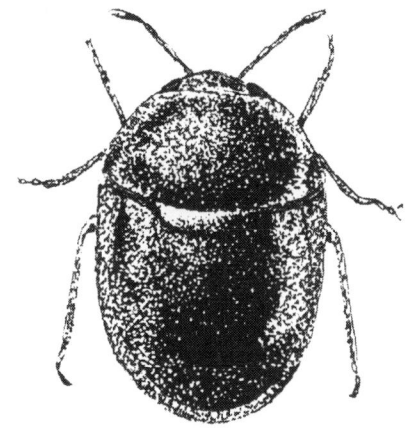

Adult body color is an irregular pattern of green and brown, they are about ¼ inch long. They have a rounded square shape. They move slowly and fly when disturbed.

Eggs are deposited on the underside of leaves. Hatching occurs in about 5 days. Development from egg to adult takes about 6 weeks.

Food includes kudzu, wisteria and related plants. The first generation of kudzu bugs feed on kudzu or wisteria. The second generation may feed on soybeans in addition to kudzu.

Habits. Over-wintering flights of adults to the sides of buildings begins in October and lasts for several weeks. They become active in early spring and move to food plants.

This bug produces an odor when disturbed. When crushed it will stain surfaces; the body fluids may cause skin irritation in some individuals. The adults fly to light colored surfaces, especially to white clothing or the side of houses. Adults over-winter in large numbers inside and outside of buildings.

Distribution of this bug is currently limited to southeastern U.S. It is expected to spread to regions where the kudzu vine grows, and this includes the Northeast and Midwest.

Spots on Leaves

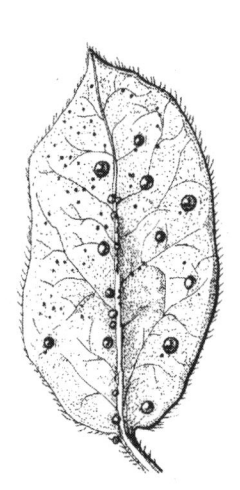

The leaves of flowering plants, shrubs, and ornamental trees may have yellow and brown spots, and dead areas along the veins and the perimeter. These are usually caused by the feeding of insects that have piercing-sucking mouthparts. Their mouthparts are inserted into the leaf surface and plant sap is sucked out; brown or yellow spots usually indicate feeding.

Spots on leaves are often blamed on insecticide spraying around ornamental plants. However, modern insecticides and solvent systems are not phytotoxic and do not cause spots on leaves.

Water Strider

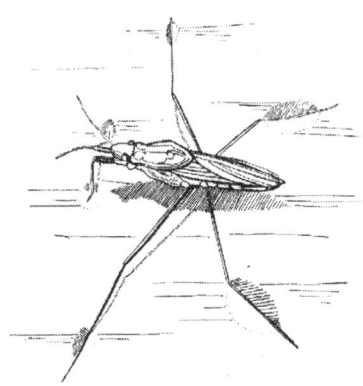

Adult is about 3/4 inch long, and brown to blackish brown. The mid and hind legs are long, the front legs are short. The adults have short wings but they are capable of flying.

Habits. These insects can walk on the surface of the water. They occur in lakes, pods, and slow moving streams. They are predators of other insects. Water striders are sometimes found in swimming pools, but they do not bite.

Backswimmer

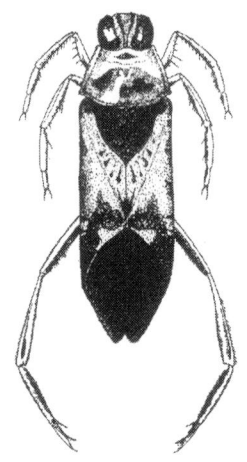

Adult is about 1/2 inch long, the body color is black to brown and sometimes shiny blue. The hind legs are long and adapted for swimming.

Habits. These bugs live in water as predators. They are fast swimmers and swim upside down. They can deliver a painful bite to people they contact in water. They are capable of long-distance flight. Backswimmers commonly occur in backyard and commercial swimming pools, even those that are a long distance from a pond or lake.

Giant Water Bug

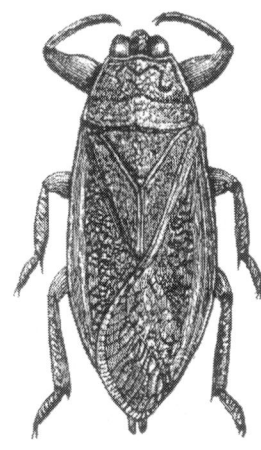

Body is uniformly brown, and about 3 inches long. The front legs are enlarged at the base, and the wings are large and overlap the abdomen.

Habits. These insects inhabit lakes and ponds where they are predators of other insects and small animals, including frogs. They have piercing mouthparts and suck the blood from their prey. They can fly long distances and can be found far from water. These bugs are attracted to lights at night, especially commercial lighting. They fly around lights making a loud buzzing noise.

Western Conifer Seed Bug

Adult body color is brown, the abdomen is banded and is seen at the sides of the wings. The antennae are banded with white. The hind legs have expanded sections that have white bands.

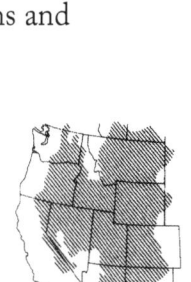

Eggs are laid on the needles and cones of evergreen trees, including spruce, pine, and fir. They prefer pine trees. Hatching is in 10 days, there are 5 nymph stages that look like the adult but lack wings.

Food includes seeds of pine cones and other conifers. The nymphs and adult shave sucking mouthparts and suck sap from the seeds.

Habits. Adults over-winter in bird nests, rodent burrows, under bark of logs and firewood. They often move indoors around doors and windows. The adults make a loud buzzing noise when they fly. They do not bite or sting.

Kissing Bugs

Adults are about 1 inch long and with an elongate head and beak. The body is are dark brown to black, the abdomen is wide and has the flattened sides sticking out beyond the margins of the wings.

Eggs are laid in cracks and crevices; hatching occurs in 8 to 30 days, nymphs develop though 5 instars. Development can require up to 3 years to complete.

Food. The name 'kissing bugs' comes from their habit of biting and taking blood around the mouth. They feed on the blood of humans and other animals.

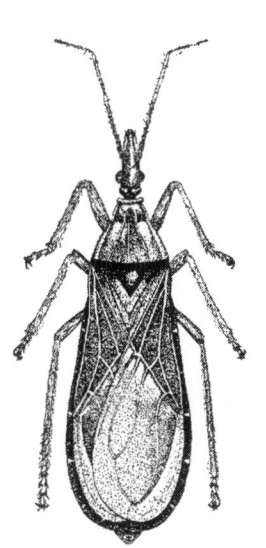

Habits. These blood-sucking insects can transmit Chagas' disease to small animals, dogs, and man. Adults are attracted to lights at night. Feeding occurs at night when the host is sleeping. The adults and nymphs are able to detect heat and carbon dioxide from their host.

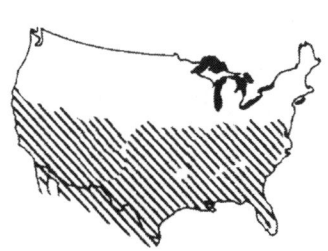

# GUIDE TO HOUSEHOLD AND WOOD INFESTING PESTS

CHAPTER 5
BEETLES

Beetles are the largest group of insects, there are over a quarter million species. The most common beetle pests indoors are those infesting stored food and natural fabric.

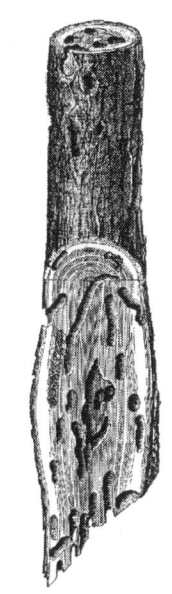

Beetles have four stages in their development: egg, larva, pupa, and adult. There can be several generations a year, especially when they are indoors. Adults and larvae have chewing mouthparts, but adults usually do not feed much and do not live long. The larval stages cause damage by their feeding. Larvae can live for months or even years as in the case of some wood-infesting beetles.

Wood is a source of food for several species of beetles. Some attack the trunk of live trees, others infest logs, and other species infest processed wood used for house framing, furniture, and flooring. Powderpost beetles can complete several generations in wood framing and threaten the stability of the structure.

Stored flour, bread, noodles and other grain products can be infested with beetles. There are several species of flour beetles that are common in households. It is almost impossible to store or process flour without having some level of infestation. Although it is the larval stages that feed on the product, it is the adult beetles that penetrate storage bins and packaging materials and spread the infestation.

Wool fabric, leather and other natural materials are attacked by several species of carpet beetles. Many of these species are called carpet beetles because of their association with carpeting that was at one time predominately made of wool.

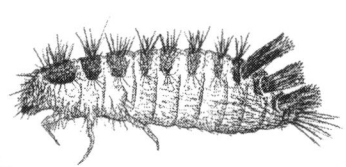

Carpet beetle larvae can eat and digest wool, leather, and animal hair. However, they are not limited to these materials, but will feed on a variety of stored food products, dead insects, and dead animals that may occur indoors or outdoors.

Anobiid Beetles

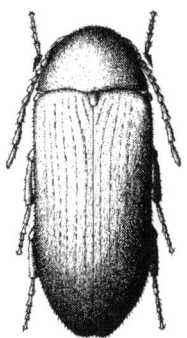

Anobiid (Family Anobiidae) infestations may be found when inspecting joists and rafters in crawl spaces, basements, and attics. Infestations can be recognized by 1/8 inch round holes with frass around the outside the holes or accumulating on surfaces under the holes. These beetle exit holes are usually the only sign of damage. The adult beetles live only a short time and the larvae are in galleries in the infested wood.

Development. Females lay eggs on the wood surface or sometimes inside an old exit hole. The eggs hatch in about two weeks and the first stage larvae immediately bore into the wood. The larvae feed for 1 to 3 years, depending on the wood moisture and age of the wood. Full grown larvae tunnel to the wood surface to pupate, and the adult beetle cuts the emergence hole to the outside.

Frass. The frass of anobiid beetles contains coarse, hard pellets, which feel gritty when rubbed lightly between the fingers.

Habits. These beetles infest all types of seasoned wood, both hardwoods (oak, maple) and softwoods (pine, spruce). However, softwood timbers used in house framing are the most often infested. Larvae can feed in wood with moisture contents as low as 10%, eggs require about 45% relative humidity to hatch.

Furniture Beetle

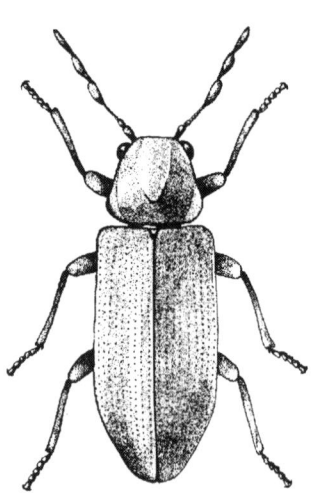

Adults are uniformly reddish brown. The wing covers have distinct longitudinal lines and the last antennal segments are enlarged.

Development. Eggs are deposited on rough wood surfaces or in cracks. Hatching is in 3-6 weeks. Larval development takes about 2 years, but can extend to 5 years. Larvae produce galleries filled with frass; they bore close to the wood surface to form a pupal chamber. Adults emerge in May or June; they live about 4 weeks.

Habits. Infestations are more common in structural pine and spruce framing wood than furniture. First-stage larva ingests yeast deposited on the egg by the female; these yeasts become established in the larval gut. Yeasts are killed at 77°F, which restricts the initial development or re-infestations of timbers in some attics.

Anobiid Powderpost Beetle

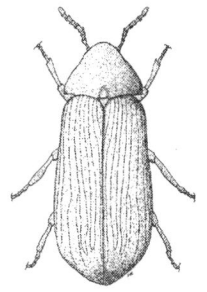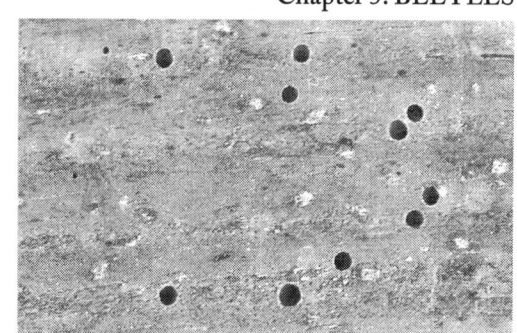

Adults are reddish brown to black. The head of the adult is bent downward. Larvae are C-shaped, pale white, and with small legs.

Development. Eggs are laid on the rough-surface of wood that is 2-5 years old. Hatching is in about 8 days. First-stage larvae immediately burrow into the wood. The larval galleries are packed with frass. Larvae reduce feeding in response to low temperatures and low wood moisture. Full-grown larvae tunnel close to the surface and prepare a pupal chamber. The life cycle is 1-5 years, depending on the wood infested.

Habits. Pine timber may be re-infested and infestations continue until nearly all the sapwood portion of the wood has been consumed, leaving only the annual rings.

Anobiid Bark Beetle

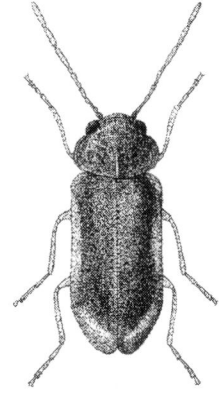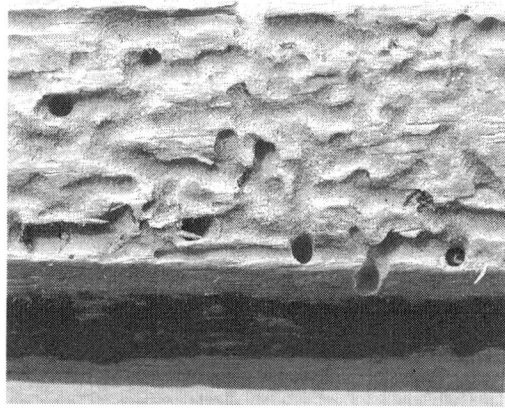

Adults are reddish brown to black. The head of the adult is bent downward.

Development. Eggs are laid in the bark. Larvae feed in tunnels between the bark and wood surface. Development takes 1-2 years.

Frass. The frass is a mixture of brown particles from the bark and white particles from the wood below the bark.

Habits. This beetle infests pine, spruce, and fir, especially lumber that has small sections of bark remaining. The damage is often confused with active infestations of powderpost beetles. This beetle does not reinfest the wood and does not cause structural weakening of lumber.

Lyctid Beetles

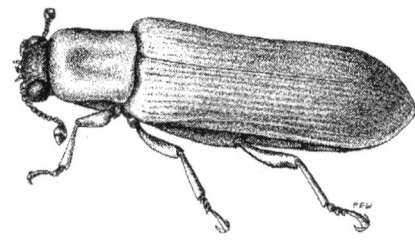

Lyctid (Family Lyctidae) infestations are in hardwoods, and usually in hardwood flooring. These beetles are also common in imported hardwoods used household molding. Infestations are characterized by 1/32 inch round holes with frass surrounding the opening (in flooring) or falling from holes. The adult beetles live only a short time and are rarely found.

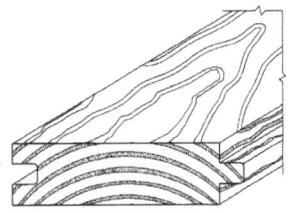

Development. Females lay eggs in exposed ends of flooring or other wood, usually in the pores of the grain or in cracks and crevices. Hatching is in about 3 weeks. Development from egg to adult requires 6 to 12 months, depending on the starch and moisture content of the wood. The life cycle extends to 2 years and as much as 4 years under unfavorable conditions.

Frass. The frass of lyctid beetles contains no hard pellets, and is soft when rubbed lightly between the fingers.

Habits. Females prefer to lay eggs in wood that is less than 5 years old because it has adequate starch content (at least 3%) for the developing larvae. Bamboo, which is a grass, has high starch content and can be infested by lyctid beetles.

Lyctid Powderpost Beetles

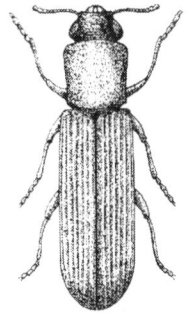

Adults are reddish brown to black; the body is distinctly flattened.

Development. Eggs are laid in cracks on the wood surface; hatching occurs in 14 days. Larval development is 8-10 months. Full-grown larvae bore close to the wood surface and form a pupal chamber. Development from egg to adult is 1 year, but can extend to 2-4 years. Adults emerge from May to September.

Habits. Larvae survive wood moisture content between 8-30%; larval development is optimum at 16% moisture content.

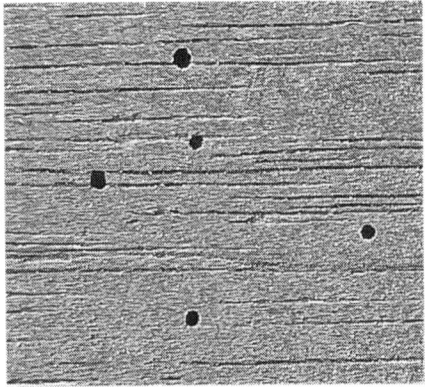

Longhorned Beetles

Old house borer and longhorned beetle damage may be found in structural wood in crawlspaces, basements, or attics. Emergence holes of these beetles are oval and about 3/8 inch long. They may be empty, plugged with fibrous pieces of wood, or contain wood powder (frass).

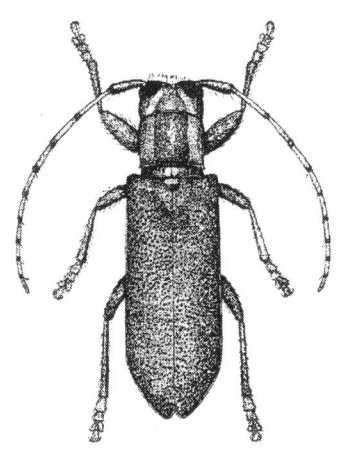

Development. Females lay eggs in crevices in the wood surface. Eggs hatch in about ten days and the first stage larvae bore immediately into the wood. Larvae feed for 1 to 3 years, depending on wood moisture. Full grown larvae tunnel to the wood surface and cut the exit hole.

Frass. The frass of most longhorned beetles is fibrous; the frass of the old house borer is powdery.

Habits. The majority of longhorned beetles attack dead and down trees and logs. They have a 1 or 2 year life cycle and do not re-infest the wood. Lumber made from wood previously infested by pine sawyers will contain the oval galleries made by the larvae. The old house borer infests only structural wood.

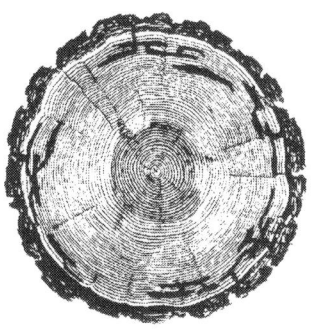

Pine Sawyers

Adults are about 1 inch long or longer; the antennae are longer than the body.

Development. Eggs are laid in crevices in the bark. Early-stage larvae feed beneath the bark, late-stage larvae tunnel deep into the wood. Larval development is completed in 1 or 2 years. Adults emerge in April and May, and are active throughout the warm season.

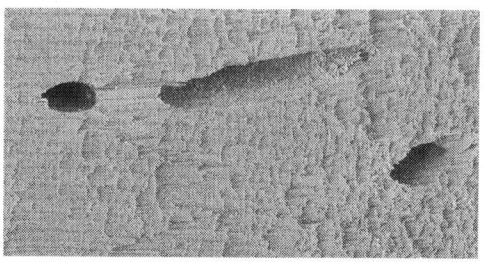

Frass. The galleries are usually empty, but fibrous frass may be found in some areas. Frass may be exposed at the wood surface.

Habits. These beetles develop in freshly cut, recently felled, dying, or recently dead trees. Larvae are called sawyers because of the sawing-wood sound they make while feeding. These beetles do not re-infest the original wood.

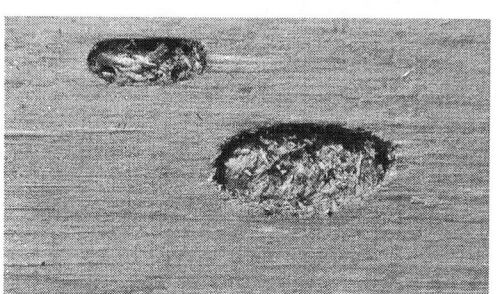

Old House Borer

Adult body is black to brownish-black; antennae are not longer than the body.

Development. Eggs are placed in cracks and crevices. Hatching occurs in about 9 days, and first-stage larvae immediately bore into the wood. Larval development takes 2-10 years. Adults live about 2 weeks.

Habits. Larvae feed on wood with moisture content of 10-20%. They do not feed on decayed wood. Infestations occur primarily in houses less than 10-years old.

Bostrichid Beetles

Bostrichid (Family Bostrichidae) beetles are primarily pests in hardwoods, but some species attack softwoods. Infestations are often in rough-cut lumber used for pallets, or in hardwood used before it is seasoned. Bostrichids do not reinfest wood after it is seasoned and the moisture content reduced. Adult beetles are 1/4 inch long and cylindrical. There is a patch of short spines on the region above the head, and there may be spines or hooks at the end of the body. Entry and emergence holes are about 1/8 inch diameter. The larval galleries are filled with powdery frass.

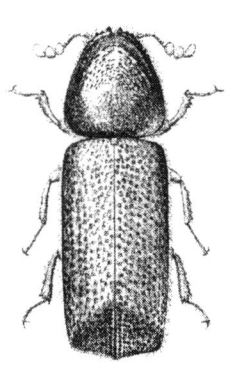

Development. Females bore into the wood surface and prepare tunnels for laying eggs. Adult beetles feed on wood as they tunnel. Eggs are laid inside the tunnels and the larvae create their own tunnels and frass as they feed. Larvae complete development in about 12 months.

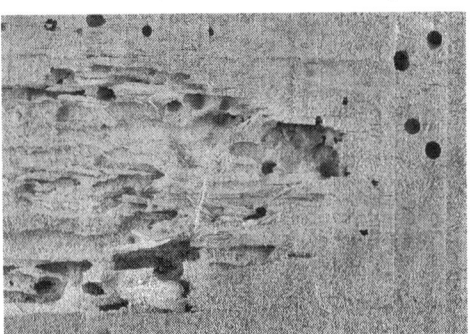

Frass. The frass is fine powder, but it does not fall from the entry or emergence holes.

Habits. They infest unseasoned hardwoods, infestations in household materials are not common. The bamboo borer infests ornamental pieces. Bamboo is a grass but has high starch content and can provide adequate food and moisture for Bostrichid larvae.

Bamboo Borer

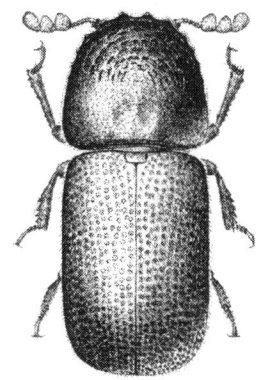

Adults are about 1/8 inch long and dark brown, the front of the thorax has numerous indentations and short spines, the head is bent downward. Larvae are pale white with a dark head.

Development. Eggs are laid in cracks and crevices in bamboo. Hatching is in about 6 days. The larval period is about 41 days; development from egg to adult is completed in 1 to 3 months. Adults live 1 to 3 months.

Habits. Infestations can occur in material made of bamboo, including furniture; stored food, flour, and spices can also be infested. The holes in bamboo may be the only evidence, the beetles are rarely seen. Infestations of stored food and flour are rare.

Oriental Wood Borer

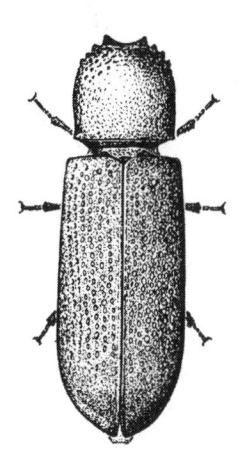

Adults are about 3/8 inch long and dark brown, the front of the thorax with numerous indentations and spines; there are two prominent spines projecting forward. The males have hooks or spines at the end of the wings. The head is bent downward and the antennae are hidden.

Development. Eggs are laid in cracks and crevices and on rough surfaces of wood; hatching is in about 7 days. Larval development period is about 6 months. The adults chew exit holes in the wood surface. Males crawl on the outside of the wood, but females usually remain in the holes to mate and lay eggs.

Habits. This Bostrichid is widely distributed in the Asia-Pacific region and can be found infesting shipments of wood materials from that region. Furniture from the Asia-Pacific region may be infested. The damage can remain hidden, but the adults (males) are often found crawling on the wood or close by. This beetle has become established in southern Florida.

Ambrosia Beetles

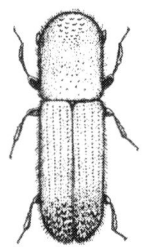

Adults are dark brown to black. The head is bent downward and the antennae are hidden.

Development. The female chews a gallery into the outer layer of wood in the host tree. Eggs are laid in secondary tunnels at right angles to the main gallery. Larvae feed on fungi growing on the walls of the tunnel. Larval development is completed in about 1 month. Adults emerge from the tree through the original entrance hole made by the female.

Habits. Damage is done to recently cut trees, including hardwoods and softwoods. Evidence of an infestation remains when wood is cut for structural timbers; the dark staining of the galleries can be seen. Pine construction timbers often have stained galleries of this beetle.

Buprestid Beetles

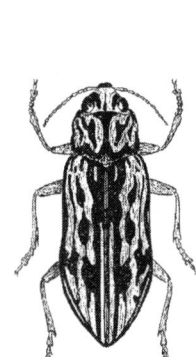

Adults are about 3/4 inch long and slightly oval; they are shiny and brightly colored. The larvae are called flat-headed borers because the body region behind the head is broad and flattened.

Development. Eggs are laid in crevices in freshly cut softwood or hardwood logs. First stage larvae bore and feed close to the wood surface, older larvae bore deeper into the wood. Development is completed in 1 or 2 years, but it may extend to 3 or 4 years in wood with low moisture content.

Habits. These beetles prefer recently felled trees rather than seasoned wood, they often come to trees immediately after they are cut. They can occur in seasoned lumber, and may be pests of modern log houses. The distinctly oval larval galleries, sometimes packed with frass, may be seen in wood siding. Solitary bees may excavate these exposed galleries as a nest site. The activity of these bees may give the false impression of an active infestation.

Cigarette Beetle

Adults are about 1/4 inch and uniformly light brown. The antennal segments are all the same size and shape, which help to distinguish this species from the Drugstore beetle, which is very similar.

Development. Eggs are laid in crevices in food material; hatching is in about 20 days. Larval development ranges from 3 to 5 months. Larvae construct silk chambers for pupation. Adults feed on the same food as the larvae.

Habits. This is a widespread pest of food materials, and is not limited to tobacco. First-stage larvae can enter small openings in the seams of food packages. Late-stage larvae are not able to penetrate smooth surfaces or cracks and crevices. Infestations are common in household food materials. Larvae feed on seeds, nuts, beans, spices, yeast, dried insects, fish, vegetables, flour, meal, and tobacco.

Drugstore Beetle

Adults are about 1/4 inch and reddish brown, the body shape is somewhat cylindrical. This species is distinguished from the Cigarette beetle by the slender shape and the enlarged segments at the end of the antennae.

Development. Eggs are laid singly in crevices of the food material. Hatching is in about 1 month. Larval development is completed in about 5 months, depending on the temperature. The full-grown larva produces a silken cocoon that is covered with particles from the substrate. This makes cocoons difficult to see in infested material. Adults live about 3 months. There are 3 or 4 generations per year.

Habits. The small size of the first-stage larvae enables them to enter openings in packaged foods. Larvae move and search for access to food material; they can survive for about 8 days without food. Infestations are common in houses and are also known from medical drugs, grain, spices, tobacco, leather, and textiles.

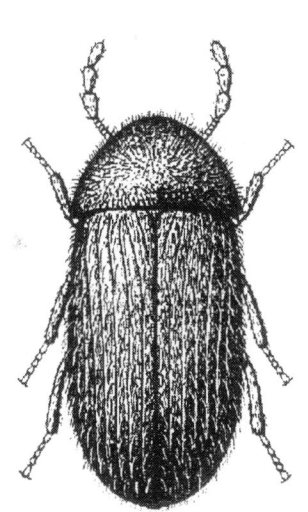

GUIDE TO HOUSEHOLD AND WOOD INFESTING PESTS

Sawtoothed Grain Beetle

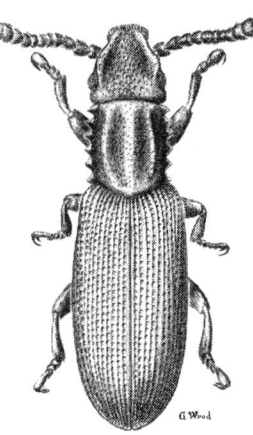

Adult is brown to reddish brown; the pronotum has 6 teeth on the lateral margins.

Development. Eggs are laid singly or in small clusters; hatching is in about 16 days. Larval development takes 12 days; larvae construct a pupal chamber from food material. Adults live for about 5 months. There are 6 or 7 generations per year.

Habits. It is the most common pest of grain, and cereal products. This is the beetle that will be in noodles, cake flour, and meal.

Red-legged Ham Beetle

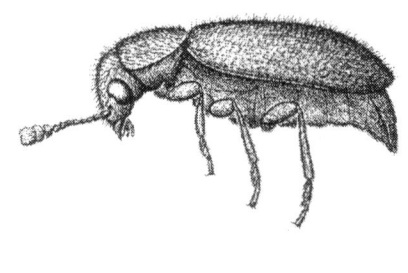
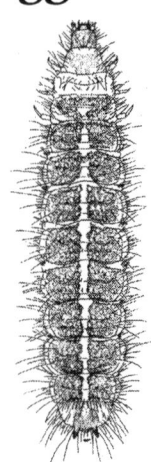

Adults are shiny green or greenish blue and have reddish brown legs.

Development. Eggs are deposited in batches of up to 28 per day. Hatching is in 4-6 days. Larval development takes about 1 month. Larvae migrate to dry locations to pupate. Adults can live about 14 months. There are 2 or 3 generations per year.

Habits. This beetle infests drying meats during long storage or a prolonged smoking process for curing meat.

Spider Beetles

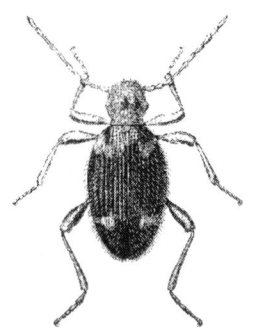
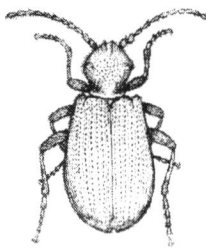

Adults have fine, yellowish brown setae covering the body. They somewhat resemble spiders.

Development. Eggs are laid over a period of 4 weeks, and females lay from 100 to 1,000. Eggs hatch in about 9 days. Larval development requires about 2 months.

Habits. Larvae pupate near the surface of infested material or crawl away to pupate. Adults are most active at night. Infested material includes nuts, beans, cacao, cayenne pepper, chocolate, corn, dried fruit, dried fish, and poultry food.

Rice Weevil

Adults are reddish brown to blackish brown. Full-grown larvae are yellowish white and C-shaped.

Development. Eggs are laid singly in grain kernels after the female bites a small hole in the surface of the kernel. Hatching is in about 6 days. No eggs are laid on grain with moisture content below 10%. Larval development takes about 26 days. Adults live 4-5 months.

Habits. This beetle feeds on beans, nuts, cereals, and cereal products such as macaroni and cake flour, rice, wheat products, and even fruits. They can occur in household cabinets infesting noodles.

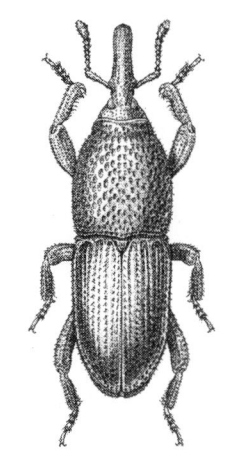

Root Weevils

Adults are dark brown to blackish brown and have a short and wide snout. These beetles do not fly. The larvae feed on plant roots. Adults emerge from May to July, and are present during the remainder of the warm season. When populations peak during spring and fall adults will enter houses and other buildings.

Habits. These short-nosed weevils can be present in large numbers around the perimeter of houses and other buildings, and sometimes move inside. Adults are attracted to lights at night, and often enter buildings through windows and doors.

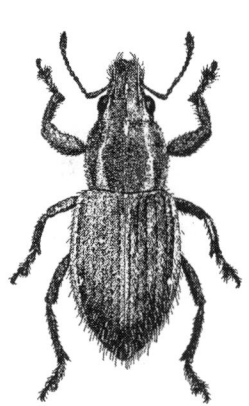

Click Beetles

Adults are about 1/2 inch long, elongate and brown, sometimes with dark spots. The antennae are long and toothed.

Development. The larvae are in soil and feed on the roots of plants. Eggs are laid in soil and larvae complete development in about 4 weeks. The adults live for several months but feed very little.

Habits. The adults can bend at the junction of the thorax and abdomen, and then snap back to a straight position. They are commonly called click beetles. These beetles will fly to indoor lights at night and are often found in houses. They will come to UV light traps.

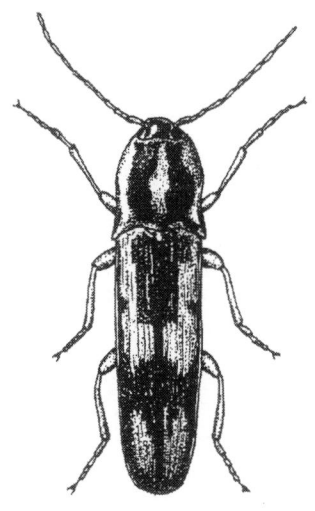

Red Flour Beetle
Confused Flour Beetle

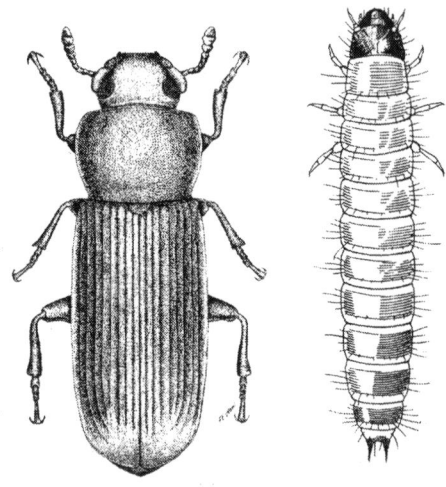

Adults of these two beetles are reddish brown. Antennae of the Red flour beetle have a 3-segmented club; Confused flour beetles have a 4-segmented club.

Development. Eggs are laid directly on flour. Larval development is completed in 19-22 days. The number of larval instars ranges from 5-11. Pupae are formed in sheltered locations in the infested material; pupal period is 4-6 days. Adults live for about 3 years, and females lay eggs for more than 1 year.

Habits. These beetles infest grain, flour and other cereal products, milk chocolate, dried milk, and hides. Adult Red flour beetles can fly short distances, but the adults of Confused flour beetles have not been observed to fly.

Yellow Mealworm

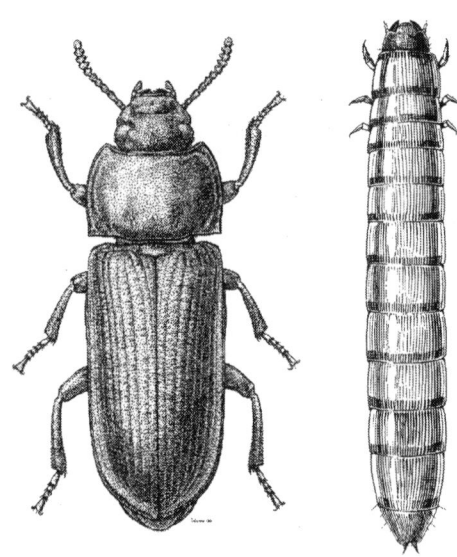

This beetle is somewhat shiny dark brown to black and about 1/2 inch long. The head and antennae are visible. The larva is shiny brownish yellow and with a hardened skin, the head is dark brown to black.

Development. Females lay about 300 eggs directly on flour or grain; eggs hatch in about 2 weeks. Larvae develop through 10-14 molts and they complete development in 10 months. The adults live for about 3 months; there is 1 generation per year.

Habits. The larvae are active at night and the adult beetles will fly to lights at night. Larvae feed on grain, animal feed, and dry pet food. Household infestations are not common, but they are known to feed on food material, particularly dry pet food hidden by mice indoors.

Furniture Carpet Beetle

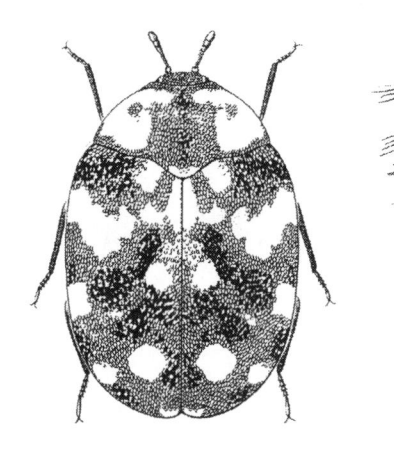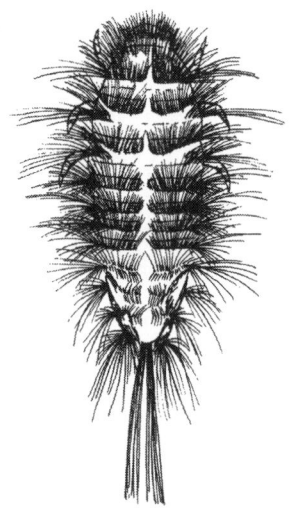

Adult body is rounded oval; there are yellow, white, and black spots scattered on the dorsal surface. Larvae are distinctly banded and with a tuft of long setae at the end of the body.

Development. Eggs are laid in batches containing up to 57 eggs; hatching occurs in 9-16 days. Larval development is 4 to 12 months depending on temperature. Development from egg to adult is 3 to 12 months, and adults live 1 to 2 months. Adults emerge in spring.

Habits. Larvae feed in a limited radius and their cast larval skins can accumulate in one place, which gives the appearance of a severe infestation. Larvae feed on wool, silk, fur, feathers, and dry animal material.

Common Carpet Beetle

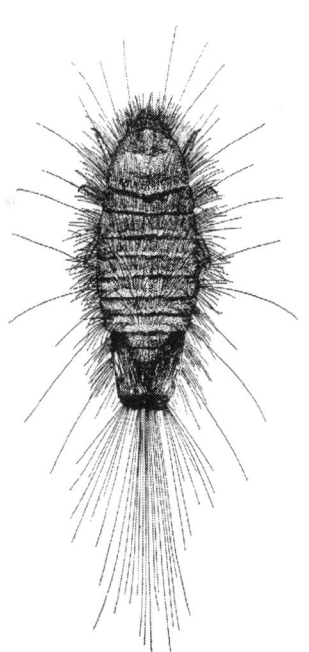

Adult body is oval, gray to black, and with a varied pattern of white and orange-red scales on the dorsal surface. Larvae are oval shaped and with long setae at the margins and a tuft of long setae at the posterior end.

Development. Eggs are laid singly or in batches of up to 36. Hatching occurs in 13-20 days. The larval development period is through about 6 instars and takes 2 to 3 months. Development from egg to adult takes about 4 months.

Habits. Larvae feed on various animal materials, including wool, feathers, hair, and fur, and museum specimens.

GUIDE TO HOUSEHOLD AND WOOD INFESTING PESTS

Varied Carpet Beetle

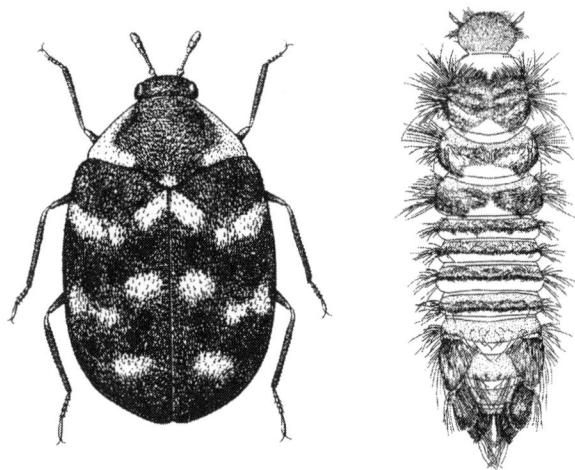

Adult body has a pattern of white, black, and brownish yellow spots. Full-grown larvae have a series of light- and dark-brown transverse stripes. At the posterior end of late-stage larvae there are tufts of setae.

Development. Eggs are deposited on larval food; hatching is in 18 days. Larval development takes 7 to 8 months, and includes 5-16 instars depending on conditions and the food material. Development is completed in 1 year. Household infestations produce adults in fall.

Habits. This species feeds on stored food materials and grain products, also in dead insects in light fixtures

Black Carpet Beetle

Adults are dark brown to black. Larvae are glossy brown and covered with brown setae at the margins; a brush of hairs projects at the end of the abdomen.

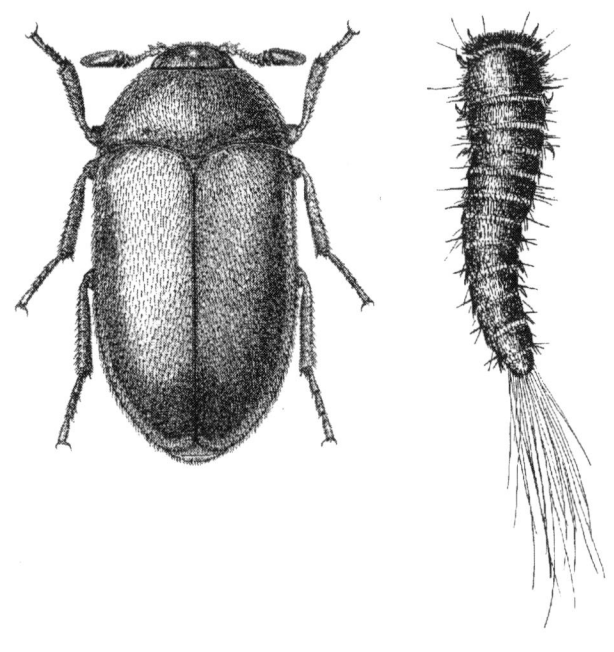

Development. Eggs are laid singly directly on the larval food, usually in late fall and winter. Hatching is in 1 to 2 weeks. Females lay about 70 eggs. Larval development takes from 9 to 20 months. Adult beetles live about 1 month.

Habits. Larvae will often crawl to the bottom of a food source or other substrate. When disturbed, larvae curl and remain motionless for a long period. Larvae feed on silk cloth, wool, feathers, hair, and fur, fishmeal, and cereal products. Larvae often bore into stored food containers.

Larder Beetle

Adult body is dark brown to black, and with a pale yellow to yellowish white band across the back.

Development. Eggs are laid singly on the larval food material; hatching occurs in 3-9 days. Development through the pupal stage takes 45-50 days. Adults live about 8 months.

Habits. Larvae typically leave the food source to pupate and often tunnel into wood. The larval stages feed on dry meat, fish, cheese, pet food, and hides. Beetles indoors can feed on the bodies of dead mice or birds.

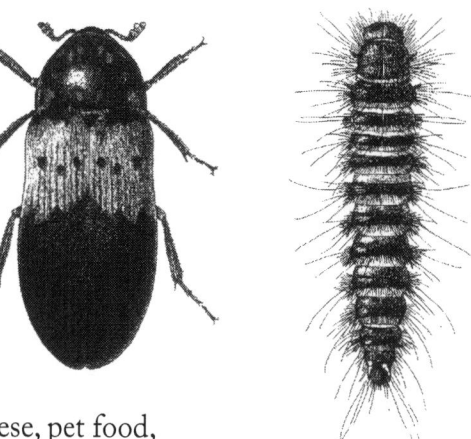

Hide Beetle

Adult body is dark brown to black, and the ventral surface is white. Larvae have numerous long setae at the edge of the abdominal segments, and on the posterior segment.

Development. Eggs are laid singly or in batches of 17-25; hatching occurs in 6 days. Larval development is about 50 days and there are 7-9 instars. Pupal chambers are constructed after the larvae bore into available surfaces. Adult beetles live about 6 months.

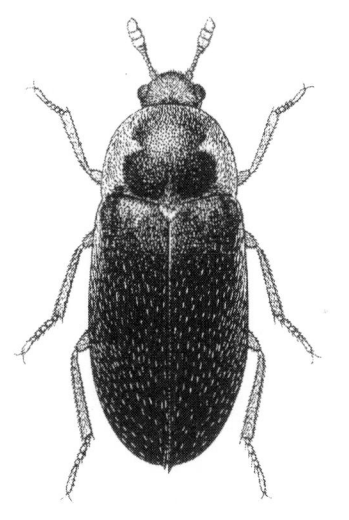
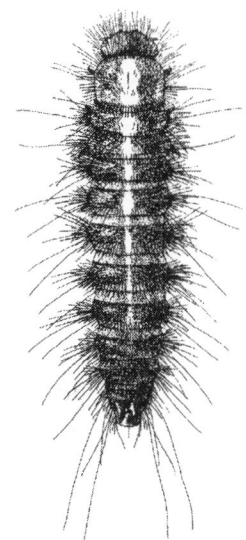

Habits. This beetle feeds on feathers, fur, bone, cheese, and dried fish. Adults are active flyers and are attracted to natural and ultraviolet light. Larvae of this beetle have been used in museums for cleaning skeletons.

Black Larder Beetle

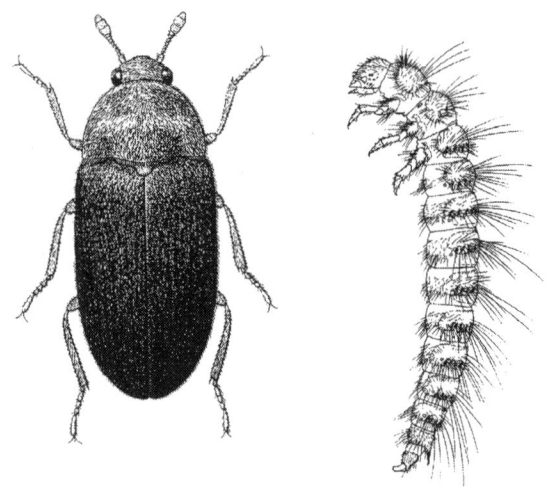

Adults are uniform black or blackish brown, and the underside of the abdomen is brown with brown spots. Full-grown larvae are dark brown and have many long hairs on their back.

Development. Larvae complete development in about 2 months and have 7-9 instars. Males and females live about 6 months.

Habits. This is a very common household pest. It feeds on smoked meat, dried fish, bones, hides, animal skins, and cheese.

Ground Beetles

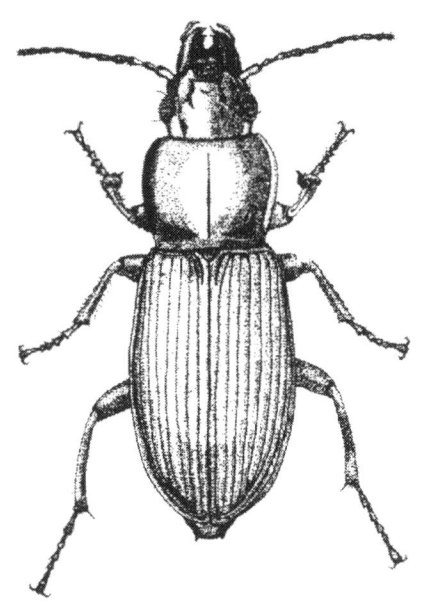

Adults are about 3/4 inch long and uniformly black, sometimes shiny. The mouthparts extend forward and the mandibles are large.

Development. Eggs are laid in soil and larvae are predaceous on ground dwelling insects. Larvae complete development in early summer and adults are active for several months.

Habits. Adults are predators of insects, particularly caterpillars. They are usually found in leaf litter, in thatch in turfgrass, and in mulch. They will come indoors around doors and windows. These beetles are very capable flyers and often come to lights at night. They are sometimes mistaken for cockroaches.

Elm Leaf Beetle

Body is yellowish green to dull green; there is a black stripe along the sides.

Development. Eggs are laid at the base of trees; hatching is in 2 weeks. Early-stage larvae climb the tree trunk and feed on the underside of the leaves. Full-grown larvae crawl down the trunk to pupate in the bark near the ground, or the soil around the tree. Larval development takes 2-3 weeks; there are usually 2 generations per year. Second-generation adults select hibernation sites in fall.

Habits. Over-wintering locations are leaf litter around the foundations of buildings, and in the attics, eaves, and interior rooms of houses. Adults usually remain active during the winter, but do not feed.

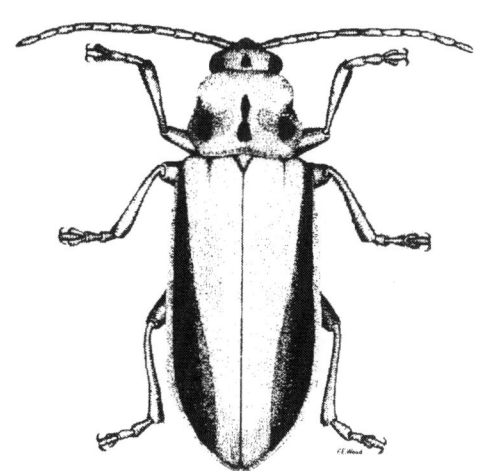

Asian Ladybird Beetle

Body color pattern varies from yellowish orange to nearly red, and they can have no spots to more than 20. Adults live several years and their color may change.

Development. Eggs are deposited in batches of 20 on the underside of tree leaves; hatching occurs in 3-5 days. Larval development is completed in 12-14 days. The pupa is attached to the leaf surface, and adults emerge in 5-6 days. There are 2 or 3 generations per year, and adults live 2-3 years.

Habits. Adults fly to natural and ultraviolet light indoors. Adult beetles select over-wintering sites on the warm sides of building.

CHAPTER 6

COCKROACHES

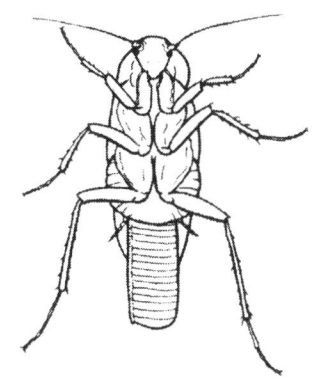

For most people the only experience they have with cockroaches are German cockroaches in kitchens or American cockroaches crawling out of sewers at night. But there are about 4,000 species of cockroaches around the world, and there are only a few pest species.

Cockroaches have long antennae and chewing mouthparts. Most adult males have wings and can fly; females often have shorts wings or none at all and do not fly. Nymphs are similar to adults except for their size and the absence of wings. Eggs are enclosed within an egg case. There are 5-12 nymph stages, depending on species.

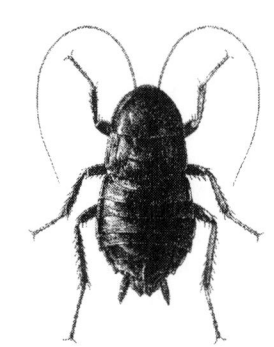

Cockroaches prefer carbohydrate foods but will also feed on material high in fat and protein. The availability of food controls their reproduction. Female German cockroaches actively forage and eat when they are preparing their eggcase, but remain relatively inactive once the eggcase is formed and during the 28 days they are carrying it.

- The habit of defecating while feeding and move about spreads pathogens to surfaces they contact.

Legs have strong spines and setae, and the small pads on the underside of their feet enables them climb. The large pad between the claws at the end of each leg helps cockroaches to move quickly on smooth and vertical surfaces.

- Oriental cockroaches do not have a large pad between their claws. These cockroaches can climb rough horizontal surfaces, but they can not climb smooth vertical surfaces. They often become trapped in sinks and bathtubs that have smooth sides. This gives the false impression they have come up the drain pipe.

German Cockroach

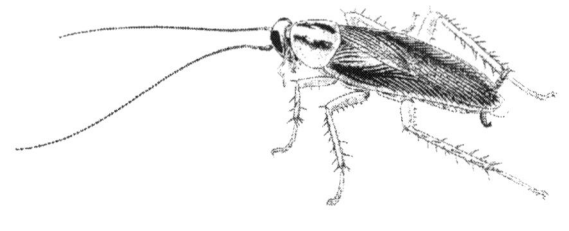

Adults are about 1/2 inch long. The body is light brown to yellowish brown. Females are slightly darker than males. Male body shape is long and slender, female shape is short and broad. There are two black longitudinal stripes on the region behind the head. Nymphs are brownish black, with a pale stripe down the center and the margins of abdomen have a light stripe.

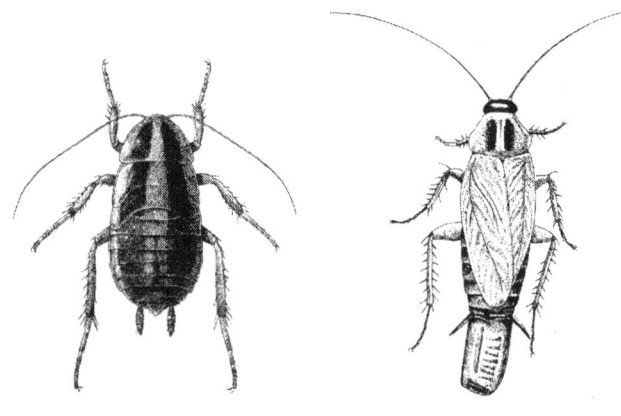

Egg case contain about 40 eggs, and hatching occurs within 24 hours after it is deposited. Females produce 4 to 8 egg cases. Development is about 6 months. There are 5-7 nymph stages in males and 6-7 in females. Adults live about 6 months.

Habits. Survival without food or water is about 8 days for males and 12 days for females; survival with water is 10 days for males and 42 days for females. Females preparing to produce an egg case leave the harborage to feed for about five days. Females carrying an egg case forage close to the harborage. Males and large nymphs forage long distances. Sticky traps containing females with eggcases indicate an infested harborage is close by.

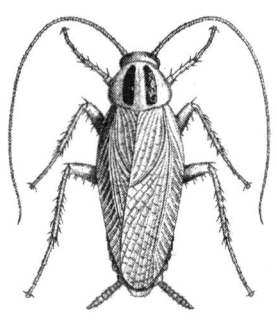

Asian Cockroach

Adults are about 1/2 inch long. The body is light brown or yellowish brown. This species closely resembles the German cockroach, but it is capable of flying. Nymphs are blackish brown, and the margins of abdominal segments are pale brown.

Egg case contains about 40 eggs. Incubation is about 20 days. Females produce 6 egg cases. Nymph development at is about 2 months. Adult males live about 45 days and females about 3 months.

Habits. They occur outdoors in vegetation; adults fly to reflected light. Flights occur at sunset and when winds are light.

Field Cockroach

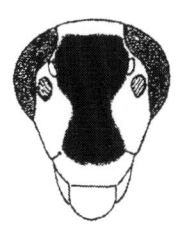

Adults are yellowish brown, and with a dark brown to black region between the eyes and extending to the mouthparts. Longitudinal stripes on the region behind the head are blackish brown. Nymphs are pale yellow; large nymphs are yellowish orange.

Egg case is light brown and with distinct indications of the egg compartments. Hatching is in about 20 days; females produce about 8 egg cases. Development takes about 2 months. Adults live 3 to 4 months.

Habits. This cockroach occurs around buildings and moves indoors during dry weather. It is active during the day, but also occurs at streetlights at night.

Pennsylvania Woods Cockroach

Adult males are slightly more than 1 inch long and females are slightly less than 1 inch long. Males and females are light brown, and the thorax and front wings have pale brown margins. Wings of male extend to the tip of the abdomen; female wings are small pads. Fames are strong flyers, but the females do not fly. Nymphs are dark brown.

Egg case is yellowish brown and it contains 32-36 eggs; about 26 eggs hatch. An egg case is produced every 5-9 days and is carried for about 3 days; females can produce 30 egg cases in their lifetime. Nymphs hatch in summer and complete development to adult in the spring of the following year.

Habits. This species occurs in woodpiles and accumulated forest debris in eastern U.S. Males can fly over 100 feet, they are attracted to lights at night in May and June. These cockroaches rarely persist indoors, they do not infest houses.

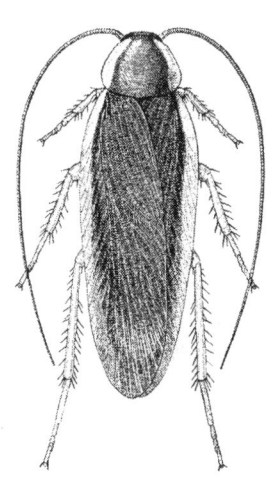

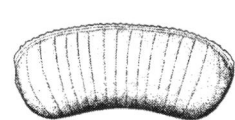

Brownbanded Cockroach

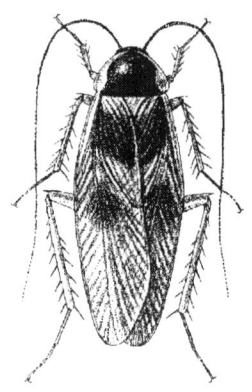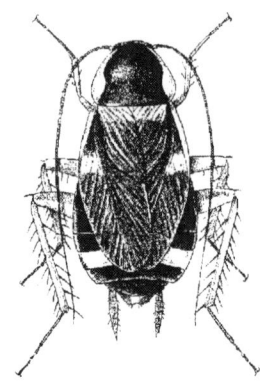

Adult males are about 1/2 inch long and females are slightly smaller. The body is brown to yellowish brown, and with distinct pale brown banding. Nymphs are banded light and dark brown. Adult males fly when disturbed, but females do not fly.

Egg case is brown to reddish brown; it is curved and there are indentations showing the position of the eggs. It contains 14-18 eggs. Hatching occurs in about 96 days. Females produce 10-20 egg cases. The egg case is deposited 24 hours after it is produced, and is glued to the substrate. Nymph development is about 4 months for males, and about 2 months for females. Adults live about 3 months.

Habits. This species is common on furniture and locations high on the walls. Eggcases are often deposited at the same location by many females. The pads on the feet of these cockroaches are small and they are not easily captured in sticky traps.

Oriental Cockroach, Waterbug

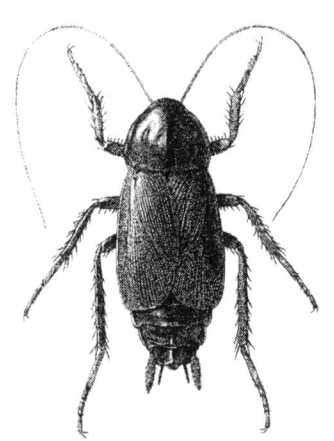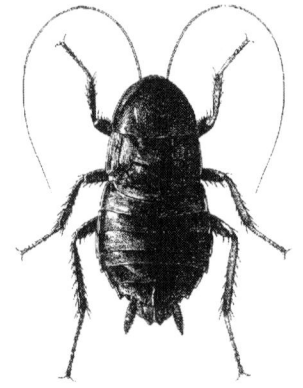

Adult males and females are slightly more than 1 inch long. Body is shiny black. Wings of male cover two-thirds of abdomen, female wings are short; neither sex is capable of flying. Nymphs are reddish brown.

Egg case is blackish brown; it contains 16-18 eggs; hatching occurs in about 42 days. Egg cases do not survive when exposed to freezing. Females produce egg cases at intervals of 1-2 weeks; the lifetime total is 6-8. Nymph development takes about 1 year for males and females. Adults and large nymphs are active from May to early July when adults and nymphs move indoors. Adults die in July or August of the second year.

Habits. Tarsi of adult females and nymphs have only a small pad between the claws; they have difficulty climbing smooth surfaces.

American Cockroach

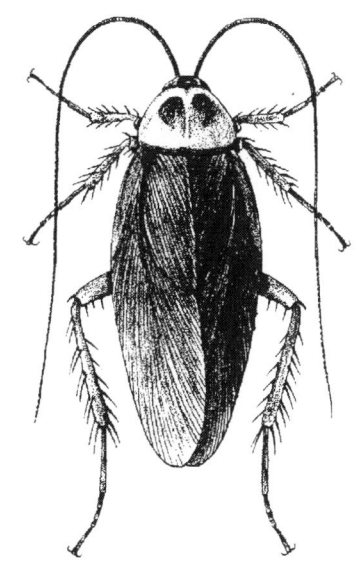

Adult males are slightly more than 2 inches long and female are about 1.5 inches long. Body is shiny, reddish brown to brown. The region behind the head has a yellowish white margin with dark brown interior. Wings extend beyond the abdomen in males, and as long as the abdomen in female.

Egg case is dark brown to blackish brown and contains about 16 eggs. Hatching occurs in about 2 months. Females produce about 15 egg cases in a lifetime; typically it is 10-15 within 10 months. Nymph development is 5-15 months. Adult life span is about 1 year.

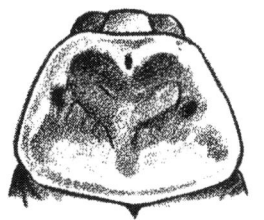

Habits. Survival without food or water is about 29 days for males and 42 days for females; survival with water is 43 days for males and 90 days for females. Adults readily fly when the temperature is above 72° F; they usually travel short distances, but sustained flight is possible. They fly to lights at night.

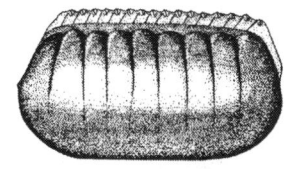

This cockroach occurs outdoors and indoors in urban landfills and wastewater treatment plants, and the underground sewer systems of cities of the world. <u>Indoors</u>, it occurs in basements, as well as on upper floors of large buildings. The female will often chew a small hole in a soft substrate to deposit her egg case, and then cover the eggcase with chewed debris so that it is partially concealed.

Seasonal abundance. American cockroach populations have a distinct seasonal abundance. Egg cases are deposited in spring and from April through July there are nearly equal numbers of adults and nymphs in the population. From August through November the number of adults decreases and the number of nymphs increases. There is relatively little foraging and feeding of adults and nymphs during winter. This seasonal abundance and foraging pattern seems to be adopted regardless of the temperature conditions in the habitat.

Australian Cockroach

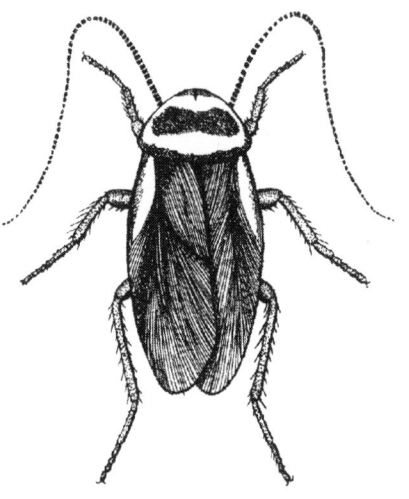

Adult males and females are slightly less than 1.5 inches long. Body is dark brown, and the region behind the head has pale margins and a dark brown interior. Large nymphs are dark brown and with pale yellow spots on lateral margins of thorax and abdomen.

Egg case is blackish brown and contains about 24 eggs. Hatching occurs in about 40 days. Egg cases are produced at about 10-day intervals, and the total is 20-30 in a lifetime. Nymph development is 6-12 months. Adults live about 12 months.

Habits. The Australian cockroach is found around the perimeter of buildings and indoors in kitchens. It occupies similar habitats as American cockroaches, but does not occur in underground sewers.

Turkestan Cockroach

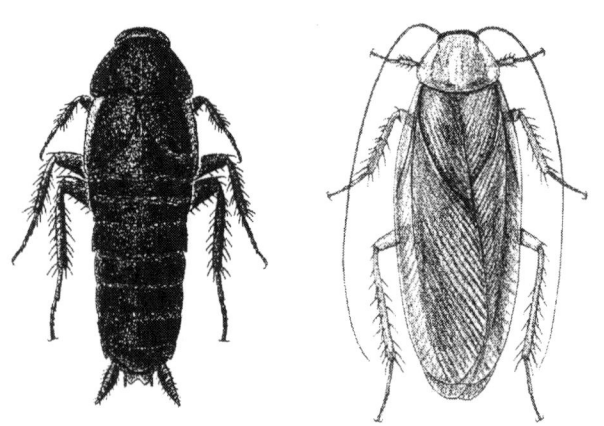

Adult males are about 1 inch long and pale brown. The wings have pale yellow margins and extend beyond the abdomen. The females are dark brown with short wings. Antennae are longer than the body.

Egg case is about 3/8 inch long and brown and contains about 18 eggs. Nymphs are have a light brown thorax and dark brown abdomen.

Habits. The Turkestan cockroach is found in southwestern U.S. as outdoor populations, but also invades houses and other structures. This cockroach can not climb. It occurs in leaf litter, potted plants, and sewer systems.

Brown Cockroach

Adults are about 1.5 inches long, dark brown to reddish brown, and the markings on the region behind the head are pale brown. Wings cover the tip of the abdomen in both sexes.

Egg case is brown and contains about 24 eggs. Females can produce about 30 egg cases, but many are not viable. Eggcases are often partially covered with pieces of debris. Nymph development is about 8 months. Adults live about 8 months or up to 20 months, depending on environmental conditions.

Habits. This cockroach occurs primarily indoors, but also lives outdoors around trees and in sewers.

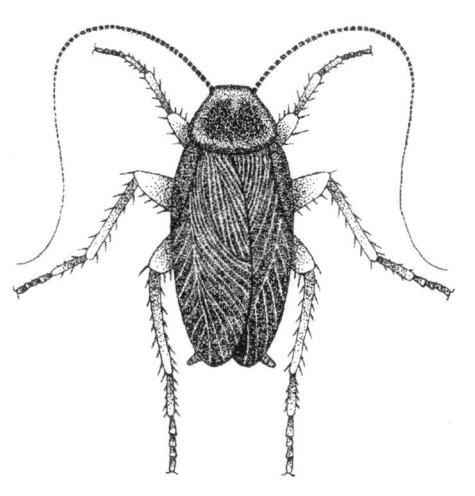

Florida Woods Cockroach

Adults are about 1.5 inches long, shiny dark brown to reddish brown. Adults have small wings that are almost indistinct. Nymphs are reddish brown and have pale yellow margins on the body. The abdomen is uniformly dark brown to blackish brown.

Egg case is brown and contains about 24 eggs; egg cases are often glued onto surfaces outdoors.

Habits. This cockroach occurs primarily in natural locations, but also in residential landscaping that includes dense vegetation. It enters houses but breeds outdoors. Adults can give off an offensive odor when disturbed. This species is sometimes called the palmetto bug.

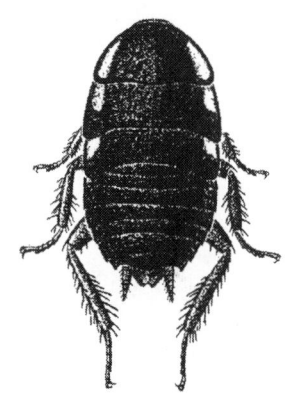

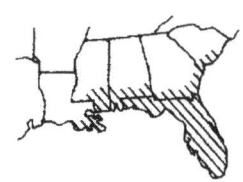

GUIDE TO HOUSEHOLD AND WOOD INFESTING PESTS

Smokybrown Cockroach, Palmettobug

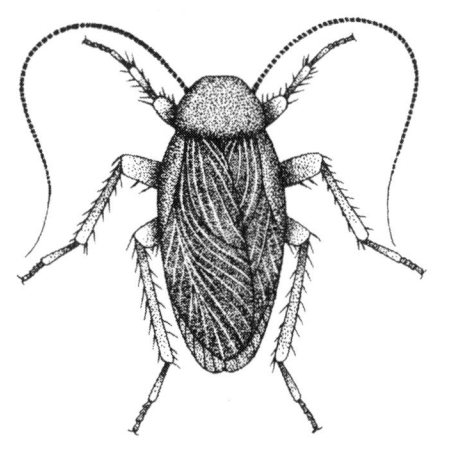

Adults are about 1.5 inches long and uniformly dark brown to blackish brown. Wings are fully developed in both sexes. Large nymphs are uniformly reddish brown.

Egg case is brown and contains 20-28 eggs. Hatching occurs in about 100 days. Females produce 15-20 egg cases in a lifetime. Nymph development is about 9 months. Adults live 18-24 months. Adults and nymphs are cold hardy and over-winter in protected sites outdoors.

Habits. These cockroaches are strong flyers, even females carrying an eggcase. Preferred outdoor habitats are moist, shaded sites, including tree holes, under bark or the bracts of palm trees, which is the basis of the name, palmettobug.

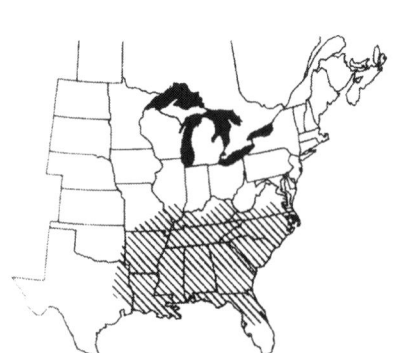

Surinam Cockroach

 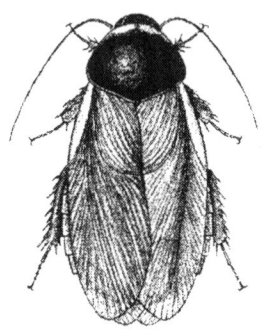

Adults are about 1 inch long; the body is dark and shiny brown to blackish brown. Wings are light brown. Wings extend to the tip of the abdomen; antennae are about one-third the length of the body. Nymphs are dark brown.

Eggcase contains 14-48 eggs and it is carried internally until the eggs hatch in about 35 days.
Development is about 4 months. Adult females live about 10 months.

Habits. It occurs in greenhouses, and occasionally around potted plants in shopping malls, hotel lobbies, and similar sites. It occurs along the Gulf coast and into coastal South Carolina and North Carolina. It is established in Hawaii.

CHAPTER 7
CRICKETS, EARWIGS, SPRINGTAILS

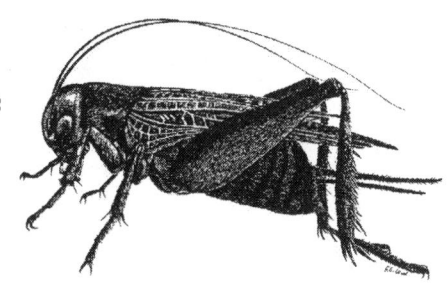

Crickets have chewing mouthparts and they are primarily plant feeders. Development is gradual, the nymph stages resemble adults. Egg and nymph stages survive dry seasons or over-winter. The house cricket is the only species in this group that lives and reproduces indoors. Other crickets come around houses looking for food or harborage, and many crickets are attracted to lights at night.

- The dry conditions indoors are not suitable for field crickets and some other species. They usually remain hidden during the day in humid locations, and most die within a week.

Earwigs have a pair of pincers at the end of the abdomen. The forceps are large in males and small in females. Earwigs have chewing mouthparts and feed on plant and animal material. They are primarily nocturnal, and remain hidden during the day. There are 4-6 nymph stages and adults appear in late summer; they over-winter as adults.

- Earwigs are attracted to lights at night, and enter buildings around doors and windows. They often gather in narrow harborages.

Springtails are wingless and soft-bodied insects. The commo from a tail-structure that they use to propel them through the air. The jumping ability helps them to escape from predators. Springtails inhabit moist locations and most feed on decaying plant material, fungi, pollen, and algae.

- The springtails that occur indoors are usually associated with moist or wet conditions, but some species can persist in dry environments. Favorable conditions indoors, include high humidity, mold, or other wet or moist organic matter. The best control strategy is to dry the site by increasing the heat in the room, or using an electric dryer.

Cave Crickets, Camel Crickets

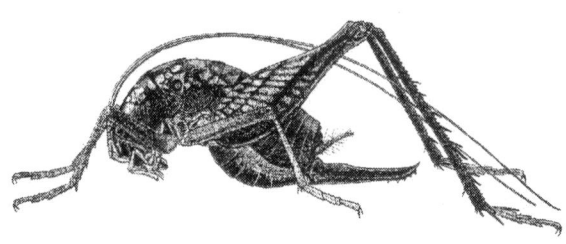

Adults are about 1 inch long, the body is light brown to dark brown, and may have a mottled color pattern on the thorax and abdomen. Antennae are longer than the body.

Development is about 64 days for males and females; there are about 6 nymph stages. Adults live about 90 days. They over-winter as immatures and adults; there is 1 generation per year.

Food is primarily plant material, including fungi and decaying leaves and roots in the crawlspace.

Habits. Camel crickets do not chirp. The common names refer to the habits of these crickets: cave cricket because they are found in dark habitats, and camel cricket because of the high arched thorax.

Jerusalem Crickets

Adults are about 3 inches long, the body is light brown to dark brown. They are wingless, the legs have sharp spines.

Development is through 9-11 molts and is completed in about 18 months. Adults appear in midsummer. Females dig a small hole in the soil to lay eggs, which hatch in the fall or spring. There is one generation per year.

Food is primarily plant material, including roots and tubers. They may also feed on dead animals.

Habits. These large crickets are often found around the perimeter of buildings, and sometimes occur indoors and in swimming pools. The human-like head of the adult has created superstitions around these crickets. In southwestern United States and Mexico they are called *nina de la tierra* or child of the earth.

House Cricket

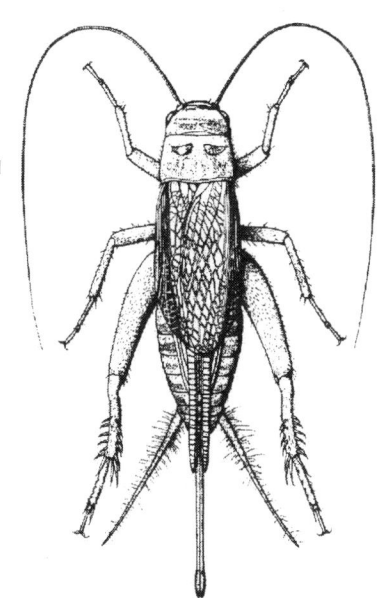

Adult body is yellowish to mottled brown and pale brown; there are 3 dark bands on the head. Eggs are deposited singly or in small batches in moist cracks and crevices; females can lay 40-179 eggs. Hatching occurs in 1-12 weeks.

Development is about 56 days for males and 53 days for females; there are 9-11 nymph stages. Adults live about 3 months. They over-winter in the egg stage and there is 1 generation per year.

Food is primarily plant material outside, and on household foods inside.

Habits. Adults are attracted to lights at night. They can climb rough surfaced buildings. They can occur in large numbers in refuse dumps and urban landfills. These sites are usually kept warm throughout the year by fermentation of wet organic material. From landfills crickets can move to surrounding buildings.

Field Crickets

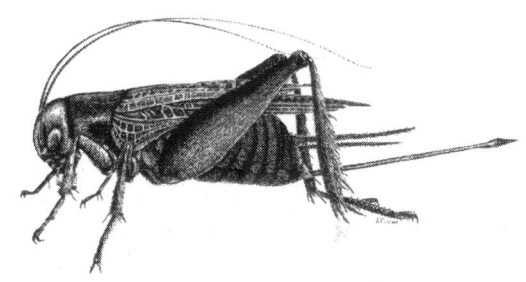

Adult body color ranges from black to yellowish brown. Front wings can have orange markings. Eggs are deposited singly in damp soil; females can lay 150-400 eggs.

Development takes 2 to 3 months; there are 8 or 9 nymph stages. Adults live for about 2 months, and in the fall they are usually killed by frost.

Food is plant material, but indoors they damage fabric, such as cotton, wool, silk, and fur. There are 1 or 2 generations per year and they over-winter in the egg stage.

Habits. These crickets are most abundant in the fall when adults gather at structures. They are attracted to lights or the sunlight heat retained by structures during the day.

Common Earwig

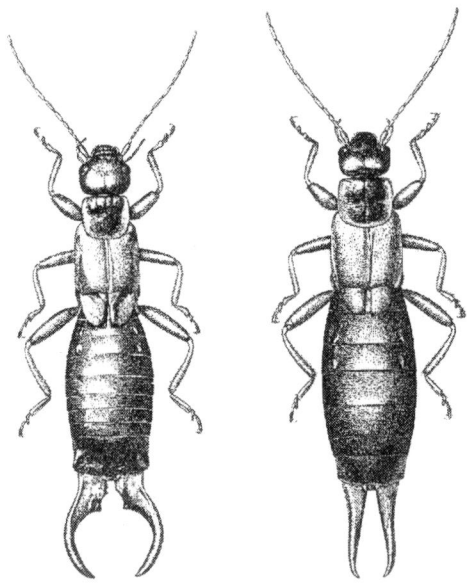

Adult body is reddish brown, and the legs are pale yellow. Males have different sized pincers, and some can be very large. Eggs are deposited in cavities in the soil, and laid in fall and/or spring to produce two generations in a year.

Development of the 4 instars is about 68 days. Adults appear in late summer. Both males and females produce an aggregation pheromone, which explains why they are often found in large groups in harborages.

Food includes a variety of green plants and insects, such as aphids, mites, insect eggs, and caterpillars.

Household Springtails

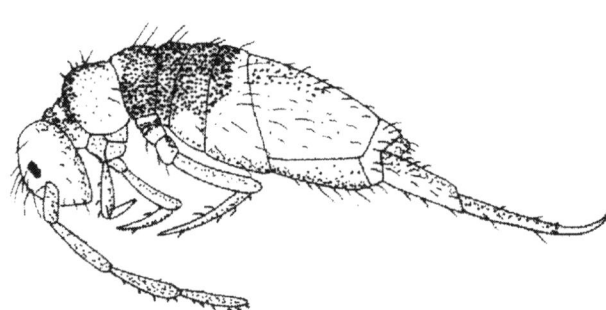

Adult body is slender and brownish black to gray, and the antennae are long. Large numbers and extensive infestations have been reported in kitchens, bathrooms, and clothes closets. Large numbers may also occur around the outside of buildings. They may be dispersed from one location to another in household materials.

Eggs are deposited singly or in small batches directly on a moist substrate. There are 6-8 molts before nymphs achieve maximum size; development is completed in about 48 days. Full-grown springtails live for about 15 days. There are multiple generations per year.

Habits. There is a tendency for gregariousness and massing of large numbers of adults and nymphs for short periods. This behavior is usually associated with abundant food, favorable environmental conditions, or migration.

CHAPTER 8

FLEAS, LICE, SILVERFISH, PSOCIDS

Fleas are laterally compressed and wingless insects. They have piercing-sucking mouthparts which enables them to suck blood from their host animal. Adult fleas are parasites of warm-blooded vertebrates.

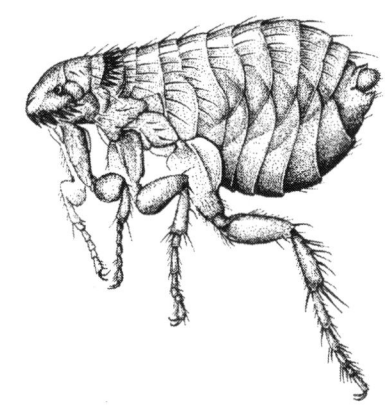

The adults remain on the body of the host. Adult fleas suck blood about once per hour, so they seldom leave the host animal. If they do, they quickly jump back to the host. Eggs are laid singly on the host, but fall to the ground. The larval stages feed and develop on the ground or bed of the host animal. Larvae resemble fly maggots.

- Flea larvae produce silk. When they have completed development the larvae will create a silk cocoon. The surface of the cocoon is usually covered with pieces of debris. The pupa forms inside the cocoon and the adult emerges by breaking open the cocoon and crawling to the surface.

Lice are wingless insects that are parasites on mammals or birds. Blood-sucking lice live on the skin of mammals and all stages suck the blood of their host. These insects are highly host specific: the dog louse is only a pest of dogs, and the human louse is only a pest of humans. They remain on their host throughout their life cycle.

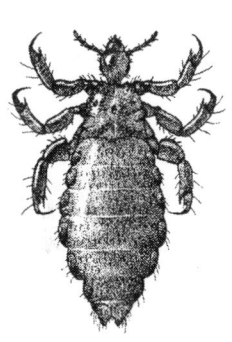

The legs of lice parasitizing humans end in a thumb and claw-like structure, which allows these insects to clinging onto hair or fibers of clothing. The shape of the claw directly influences their ability to infest different races. In the United States the prevalence of head lice infestation is 35 times higher among the Caucasians than among the Black portion of the population.

Silverfish are common in households around the world. They are well adapted to live in the dry conditions found indoors. They can feed on a variety of plant materials, and can be found in kitchens and bathrooms. The four-lined silverfish can be found throughout infested structures including basement, wall voids, and attic.

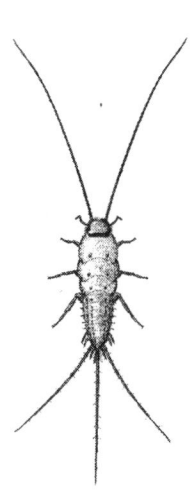

- Infestations of four-lined silverfish are usually large in houses with wood-shingle roofs.

GUIDE TO HOUSEHOLD AND WOOD INFESTING PESTS

Cat Flea

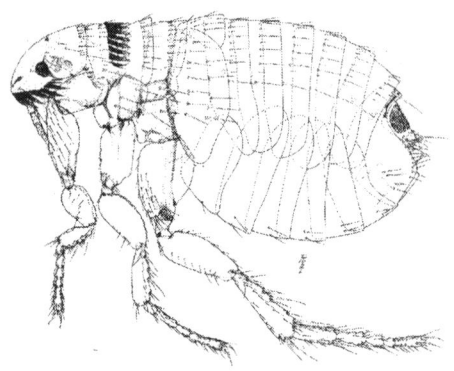

Adults are brown to yellowish brown; males are slightly smaller than females. Full-grown larvae are yellowish white, but may be reddish brown after feeding on dried blood.

Eggs are smooth and shiny. About 70% of the eggs fall from the animal within 8 hours, usually when the host shakes or scratches. Eggs are found at sites where the infested animal sleeps or rests. Hatching occurs in about 48 hours. Females lay 40-50 eggs per day; total number produced is 300-800 eggs.

Larval food is organic matter and dried blood feces of the adult flea. Larvae complete development and pupate within 1 month of egg hatch. Emerged adults may survive for 3 weeks if a host is not available, and may live for about 4 months on a suitable host. Mechanical pressure, vibration, and heat will stimulate the emergence of adult fleas from the cocoon. Walking onto carpet infested with fleas usually provides the vibration and pressure to trigger hatching and adult fleas attaching and biting ankles and lower leg regions.

Habits. This species is found primarily on domestic dogs and cats worldwide. It also infests feral mammals in urban areas, including opossums and skunks. The cat flea is much more common than the dog flea, and it occurs on both animals.

Adult fleas on animals are usually most common at the base of the tail and on the head, places where the blood flow in close to the surface of the skin. When they are indoors, recently emerged fleas will attempt to feed on humans. Human skin is difficult to penetrate for fleas, but they may try several times. Flea bites on people often occur in a line of three or more bites.

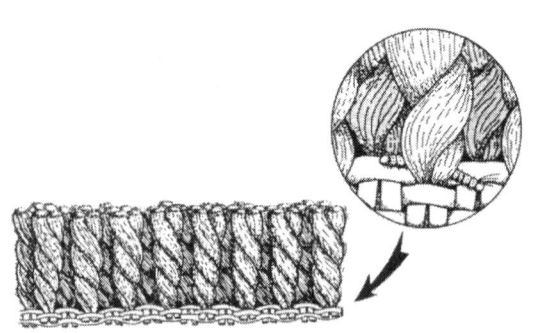

Distribution. The location of cat fleas indoors is linked to behavior of the infested pet dogs or cats. Sites where animals sleep or rest have accumulations of dried blood feces from adult flea feeding. These sites have large numbers of cat flea eggs and larvae, corresponding to the where the dried blood falls to the floor.

Head Louse

Adult body is gray to translucent, but usually resembles the hair color of the host. Nymphs resemble the adults. Adults and nymphs live and feed on the body of the host. They are usually found on the neck and head, particularly behind the ears and on the back of the neck. Eggs are glued to hairs on the head and neck.

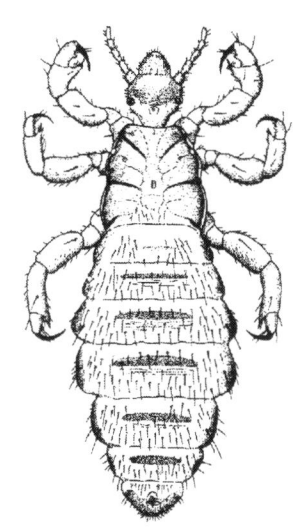

Eggs are yellowish white. Females attach eggs singly, close to the base of a host hair. Hatching occurs in 7-10 days. Females lay about 7 eggs in 24 hours, and lay a total of about 55 eggs in a lifetime. Scalp hair grows every day, and as it grows, the egg or nit is moved progressively farther and farther from the scalp. Immature development is completed in 8-9 days. Males and females live about 10 days; adults and nymphs survive about 2 days away from the host.

Spread is usually by the exchange of clothing with stray hairs with eggs or lice attached, or by close and prolonged physical contact. Lice on school children are a common condition around the world, and often wrongly associated with neglect or unclean conditions at home.

Silverfish

Silverfish are slender, flattened and tapered, and they have three tail-like appendages at the end of the abdomen. Their body is covered with shiny, fish-like scales, which is the origin of their common name. Mouthparts are the chewing type. Development progresses through many stages. They are long-lived insects.

These insects are scavengers. Indoors they feed on starchy material, including old-book binding, starched clothing, and starch-based wallpaper glue. They often occur in large numbers in attics of houses with wood-shingle roofs. Firebrats will attack knitted or plain weave fabric. The firebrat can digest starch, fat, and protein. The four-lined silverfish can digest cellulose material.

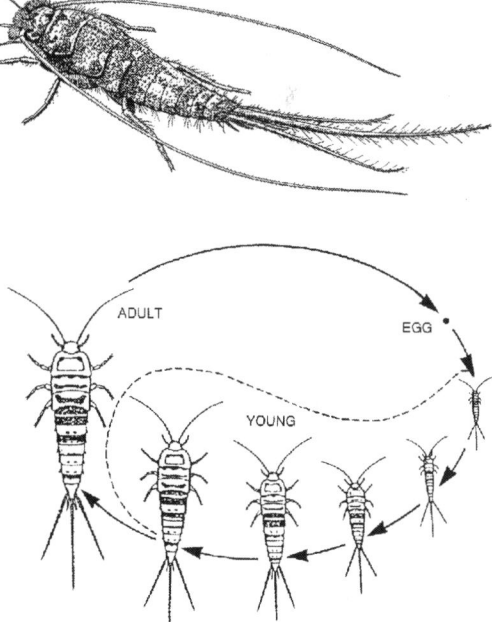

Common Silverfish

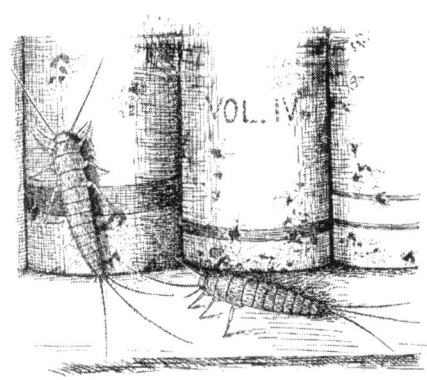

Adults are about 1 inch long, not including the long terminal appendages. They are silver-gray, with a metallic sheen.

Egg production is about 100. Development from nymph to adult takes 3 to 4 months. Adults live about 3 years.

Habits. Food is usually carbohydrates and protein material. In food storage areas they feed on flour, meal and other similar products, cotton and silk fabrics are also attacked.

Firebrat

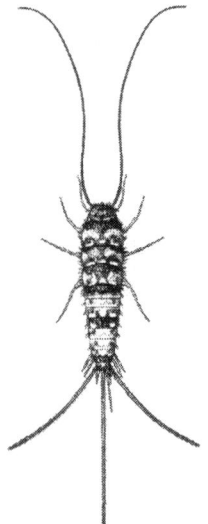

Adults are silver-gray, with a somewhat mottled gray appearance.

Egg production is about 50 eggs. Development is through a long series of molts. There are about 13 days between successive molts, and individuals have 45-60 molts in a lifetime. Adults live about 2 years.

Habits. Firebrats prefer indoor locations with temperatures above 89° F; optimum development occurs between 98-102° F. They are pests in commercial locations that maintain high temperatures, such as food processing plants, and equipment rooms.

Cereal and Household Psocids

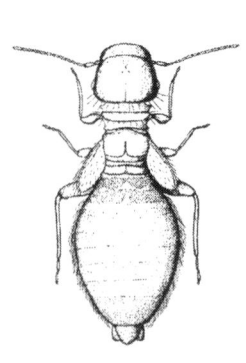
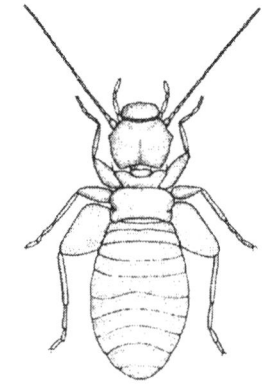

Adult have a brown body and the abdominal segments are striped.

Eggs are laid in batches of 2-3 daily; females produce about 200 eggs. Development is through 4 nymph stages over 1 to 2 months. This species does not develop in locations that have less than 55% relative humidity.

Habits. They are common pests of food storage facilities and retail food stores, in both locations infestations may occur on pallets, within packaging, and in the product. In retail stores this species is common in flour, cereal products, and sugar.

CHAPTER 9

FLIES

Flies are active during the day, and they are usually inactive at night. Adult flies eat only liquids and prefer sugar-based liquids. The larva is the primary feeding stage. Female flies lay eggs on a suitable food source for the larvae, and larvae remain in the food until they complete development. Food eaten by fly larvae includes plant and animal material, some fresh, some partially decayed, and some rotting.

Female flies are attracted to the odors produced by decaying plant or animal material that will be a suitable food for the larvae. Fruit flies are attracted to decaying fruits and vegetables, house flies are attracted to the odors produced from garbage, and blow flies and phorid flies can detect the odor of decaying animals from a long distance.

Flies are active during the warm an humid months of the year, and are inactive during the cold months. This is noticeable in the seasonal abundance of the house fly and mosquitoes. House fly populations develop slowly in spring and are most abundant in the fall. Adults live about a month, and they are abundant in late summer. Mosquitoes usually have a population peak in the spring (June) when there are pools of water available for development, and a second peak in fall (September)

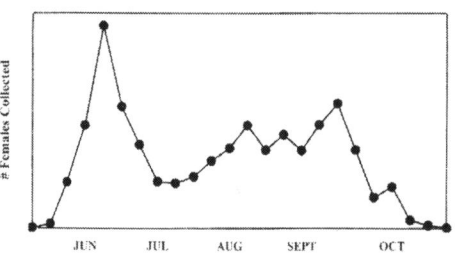

Adult flies live about 30 days and during that time they will lay a large number of eggs. Female mosquitoes take frequent blood meals during their life time, and this food is converted into eggs.

Mosquitoes breed in standing water that may occur in discarded containers or small pools. Female mosquitoes are capable of flying a long distance to find a blood meal.

- The Asian tiger mosquito frequently breeds in small amounts of water around houses and other buildings. This species is active in late spring and throughout the summer; sometimes there is a second peak of activity in the fall.

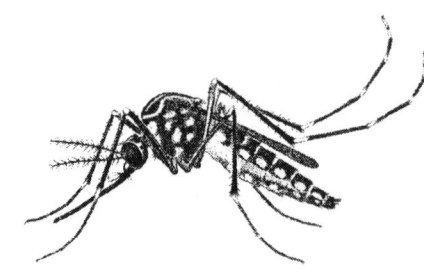

Blow Flies

Blow flies are large blue and green colored flies that are attracted to kitchens and garbage and dumpster stalls. These flies are easily recognized by the bright shiny color, and their buzzing at windows.

All blow fly species have the same basic life cycle: egg, three larval instars, a brown puparium containing the pupa, and eventually the adult. They complete their life cycle in 10-20 days, depending on temperature. These flies develop in decaying organic matter and substrates with high protein content. Decomposing animal carcasses are a common breeding site.

Blue Blow Fly

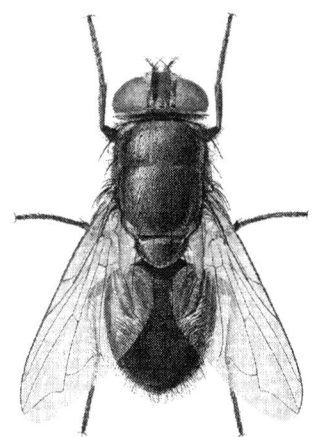

Adults have a bluish-black thorax, and a metallic-blue abdomen.

Development. Eggs are laid in batches of up to 180 directly on the larval substrate; females can produce 500-700 eggs. Hatching is in about 20 hours. Larval development is completed in about 3 days during the summer. Adults live about 30 days. Females lay eggs on fresh, decaying, or cooked meat, and on human excrement.

Habits. Adults appear in early spring, but there may be a peak of adults in fall because the adults that emerged in late summer will live for about 30 days. These are slow flying and loud-buzzing flies, and they often enter houses.

Green Blow Fly

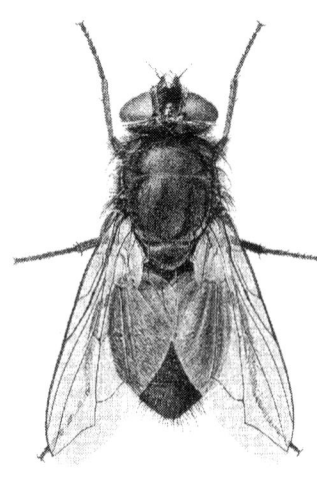

Adults are metallic green. Full-grown larvae are about 1/2 inch long and may be colored slightly purple.

Development. Eggs are deposited in large numbers in one location; females can lay a total of about 250 eggs. Hatching occurs in about 24 hours. Larval development is completed in about 5 days.

Habits. This fly breeds in dead animals, decaying garbage, and manure. Green blow flies are common in and around houses, and adults can enter openings as small as 1/8 inch. Larvae will develop in dead birds or rodents in attics and wall voids.

Cluster Fly, Attic Fly

Adults have a broad thorax covered with golden-yellowish setae; the wings overlap when at rest.

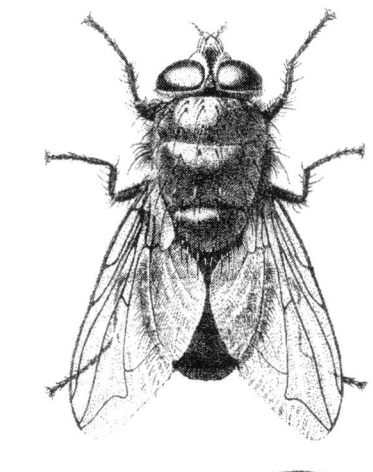

Development. Eggs are laid singly in the soil, and hatching occurs in about 3 days. Larvae attack and feed on earthworms. Larval development is completed in about 1 month. There may be 4 generations per year.

Habits. In late summer and fall, large numbers of adults gather on the sun-warmed sides of buildings, and then move through cracks and crevices to enter the attic space and wall voids. They remain there throughout the winter. In early spring adults leave during warm and sunny days.

Fruit Flies

Fruit flies gather around ripe and decaying fruit and decaying vegetation indoors and outdoors. The small size of the adult gives them access to food sources unavailable to some other flies, but their weak flight limits their activity to protected locations. There are about 10 species associated with man-made habitats. *Drosophila melanogaster* is a fruit-feeder in the larval stage; *D. funebris* breeds in organic waste, including feces.

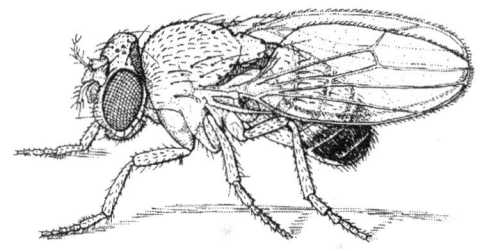

Adults are attracted to compounds that are found in fermenting material. Under ideal conditions adults live about 40 days. Females begin laying eggs 2 days after emergence. Females lay eggs directly on the larval feeding substrate, which may be wet or liquid.

House Fly

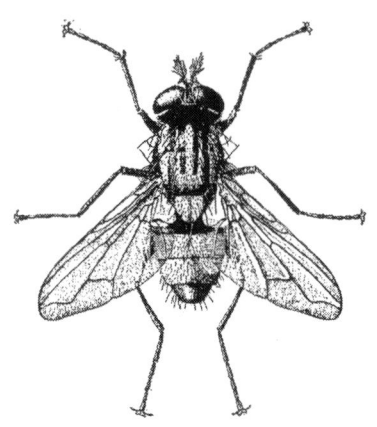

Adults have four light stripes lengthwise on the thorax. Full-grown larvae are yellowish white.

Development. Eggs are deposited in batches of 75-150; females may deposit as many as 21 batches of eggs for 31 days. Eggs hatch in 8-12 hours. Larval development is completed in about 5 days, and full-grown larvae move to a dry substrate before pupating. Adult flies live about 30 days during warm months, but this may extend to 60 days.

Habits. The usual distance traveled by adult house flies is about 1300 feet. Adults are active during the day, which are the hottest and driest portions of the day. Adults are attracted to artificial light during the day or night.

Phorid Fly

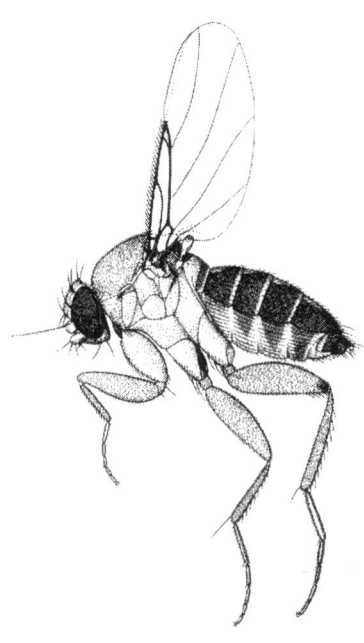

Adult body is yellowish brown; the abdominal segments are yellowish brown. Full-grown larvae are pale yellow. The puparia are brown and have two distinct 'horns' on the anterior surface.

Development. Eggs are usually laid at the edge of the substrate, and females lay eggs for about 30 days. The total number of eggs laid is about 600, but can be as many as 1,000. Hatching occurs in about 24 hours. Larval development is complete in about 3 days. Total development time is about 13 days.

Habits. Adults are found close to the breeding site and often at windows and lights near the site. The larvae of these flies feed in decaying plant and animal matter, including sewage and household organic waste. Phorids are often found in hospital and health care facilities, where they infests organic substrates, such as human waste.

Fungus Gnats

Adults have a black body; the wings are nearly black. Larvae are white and slightly transparent, the head is black.

Development. Eggs are deposited in crevices in batches of up to 30 eggs; females lay a total of about 175 eggs. Hatching occurs in about 7 days. Laval development is completed in 2-3 weeks. Adults live about 10 days and feed on moisture in the soil.

Habits. Fungus gnats occur indoors in the moist or wet soil used for potted houseplants. Mating is on the surface of moist, organic substrates; there are no mating swarms.

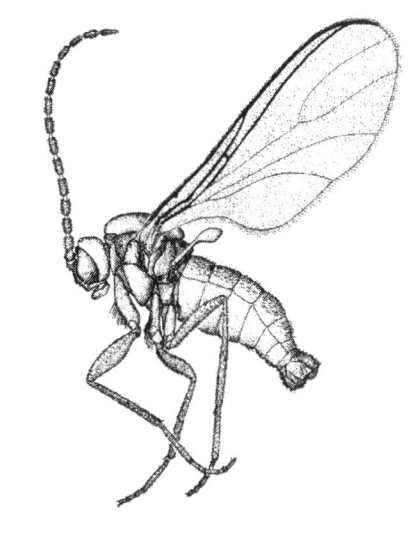

Drain Fly

Adults are uniformly gray and covered with fine setae or hairs. Full-grown larvae are yellowish white to light brown. There are dark areas on the top side of all the larval segments. The larva head is dark brown and the last segment of the body is elongated and dark brown to black.

Development. Eggs are laid in batches of 20-100 directly on decaying substrates. Hatching occurs in about 48 hours. Larval development is complete in 9-15 days. Adults are weak flyers; indoors they rest on walls close to the breeding site. They are not attracted to lights at night, and may not come to UV light traps.

Habits. Females search for egg-laying sites. The most common sites are clogged drains and the organic material around fixtures in bathrooms and kitchens. Treating the clogged drain with various chemicals rarely controls these flies. The best control strategy is to physically remove the clogging material and then maintaining the drain with biocleaners.

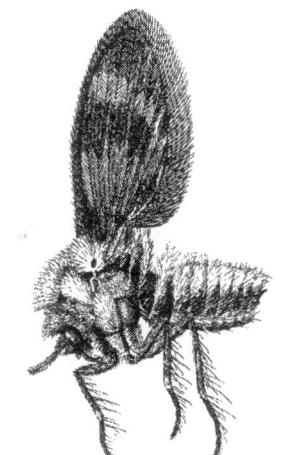

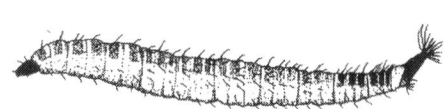

Redtailed Flesh Fly

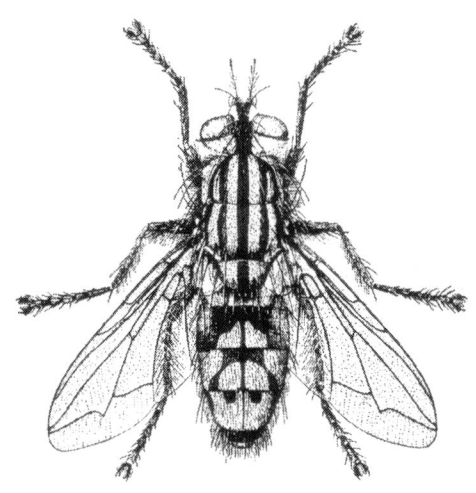

Adult body is blackish gray; with 3 dark stripes on the thorax and a black and gray checkerboard pattern on the abdomen.

Development. Eggs develop within the female's body and she is able to deposit first-stage larvae directly on substrates. Larval development is completed in about 6 days, and the pupal period lasts 8-10 days. Adults live about 30 days and there are several generations per year.

Habits. Large numbers of adults may occur indoors if larvae have been feeding on the body of a dead animal, in a wall void or chimney.

Crane Flies

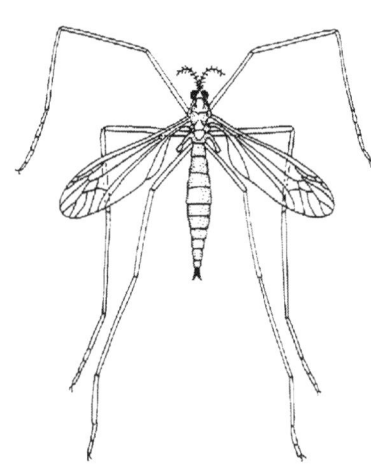

Adults are brown to grayish brown. Their wings are spotted brown, and usually slightly transparent. The adults do not feed and live for only a few days.

Development. Larval development is in leaf litter and wet organic material. Some species breed in the thatch layer in turfgrass. Adults emerge in spring and begin laying eggs soon after they fly. There are 2 or 3 generations per year. Adults are most often found in spring or early summer.

Habits. These flies are common in urban and rural areas, and they are sometimes considered large mosquitoes. They are harmless. These flies often come to lights at night and will occur indoors around lights.

Midges

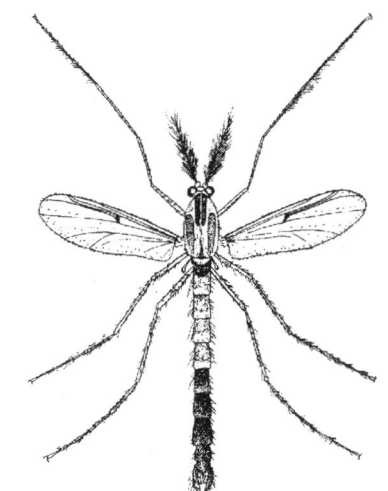

These flies are about 1/2 inch long and have a gray to black body. The wings are clear and the antennae are large and bushy.

Development. Larval development is in ponds, lakes and slow moving rivers, where they feed on plant material. Larvae complete development in about 3 weeks and the adults emerge to fly for only about 4 days. The adults do not feed. They die soon after mating and laying eggs.

Habits. Swarms of these delicate flies are common in spring and fall. They are often attracted to lights at night and sometimes fly indoors. They are mistaken for mosquitoes. Adult midges have no mouthparts and can not bite.

Mosquitoes

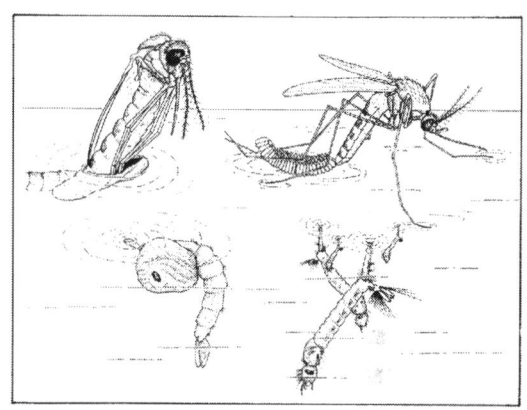

Males remain close to the breeding site and do not bite; females may fly long distances to find a blood meal. They seek wet or aquatic sites to lay eggs. Larval stages are aquatic.

Development depends on temperature, and ranges from 7 days to 7 months. For most species there are 2 or 3 generations per year. Some over-winter as unfed females, some in the egg stage.

Asian Tiger Mosquito

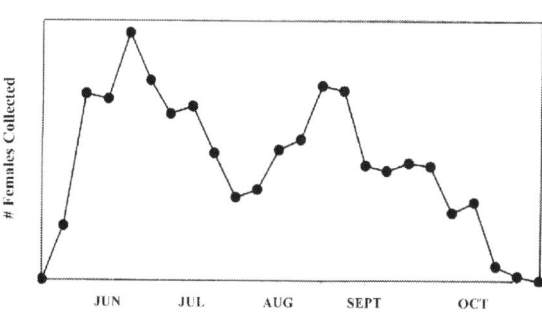

This is a day-biting mosquito, with peak biting early morning and late afternoon peak. Females can travel a mile or more from the breeding site to find a blood meal. This species breeds in containers and small collections of water around buildings.

 GUIDE TO HOUSEHOLD AND WOOD INFESTING PESTS

Common House Mosquitoes

These mosquitoes typically begin flying and biting people at dusk, and remain active until after sunset. They may not fly when there is moderate to strong wind. They readily come indoors through open doors and windows. The breeding sites are usually close to the house, and include clogged gutter (holding water), and small containers that hold water. Females can travel long distances for a blood meal, but usually remain close to the breeding sites around houses. Populations begin slowing in spring, but remain active throughout summer and fall.

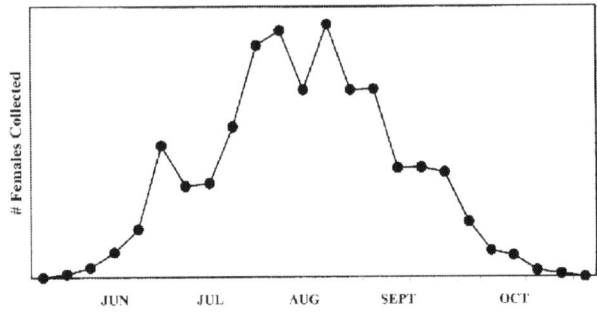

CHAPTER 10
MOTHS

Caterpillars of several moth species are pests of wool, silk, flour and cereal products. It is the caterpillar stages that feeds and damages products; the adult moth does not feed. Eggs are deposited directly on the food source of the caterpillar stages. Hatching occurs in several days, and development is completed in 1-3 weeks. Number of caterpillar stages ranges from 5 to 8.

Full-grown caterpillars move away from their feeding site to form the cocoon and then the pupa. Caterpillars have silk glands that open at their mouth; they use silk to make feeding shelters and to wrap and protect the pupal stage. Pupae of most species are encased in a silken cocoon.

Stored food pests can penetrate the seams and small openings in modern packaging material. The species that attack wool and silk fabric are easily moved to other locations in infested material. Most of the flour and grain pests have been distributed around the world with commercial shipment of food and materials.

- Moth pests of stored food can be detected with sticky traps that use a pheromone as an attractant. Pheromone traps release a female sex pheromone or male aggregation pheromone that attracts only males in the vicinity. Males detect low concentrations of this chemical and fly toward the source.

Clothes moth caterpillars may create holes in fabric made of silk or wool. They do not feed on cotton fabric. However, caterpillars will feed on some food stains in fabric, and this feeding will result in holes. Carpet beetle larvae will also attack natural fibers and create holes in the surface.

- Holes in cotton fabric may be caused by the teeth of the zipper on a garment hooking into a thread during washing.

Angoumois Grain Moth

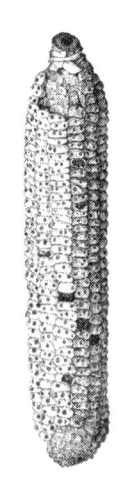

Adult wingspan is about 1/2 inch; the body is grayish to yellowish brown. Full-grown caterpillars are about 1/4 inch long, and their body is white with a yellowish brown head.

Development. Eggs are laid directly on the surface of food; females can produce 80-200 eggs. Hatching is in about 10 days. Caterpillar development is completed in about 21 days, and total development time is about 40 days. There are 4 or 5 generations per year, but in heated buildings there may be 10-12 generations.

Habits. Caterpillars attack stored whole grain or caked grain in containers. In households, ears of ornamental corn (Indian corn) may become infested. The adults typically remain near infested material will take flight in large numbers when the material is disturbed.

Indian Meal Moth

Adult wingspan is about 1 inch; the wings are pale gray, and the outer portion of the forewing is reddish brown. Full-grown caterpillars are about 1/2 inch long and yellowish white, but may be greenish or pinkish white.

Development. Eggs are deposited in the food; females lay 150-400 eggs. Hatching is in 4-5 days. Caterpillar development is completed in about 60 days. Full-grown caterpillars move away from the infested site to pupate; they wander for many hours and a long distance before stopping to make a cocoon.

Habits. Adults are weak flyers, and remain at rest for long periods on walls. Caterpillars are often found crawling on walls and ceilings near or some distance from the infested material. They are often misidentified as maggots. The adults may remain close to the infested site; they typically fly short distances and then rest. They are not attracted to lights at night.

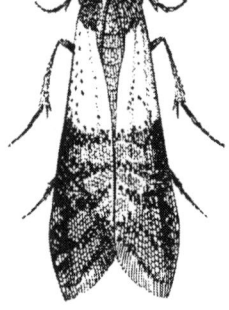

Meal Moth

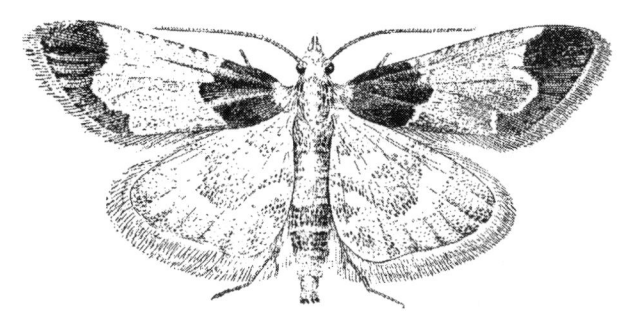

Adult wingspan is about 1 inch. The front wings are light brown in the middle and dark brown at the base and the tip. Caterpillars are about 1 inch long, the head is black and the posterior is pale orange.

Development. Eggs are scattered on the food surface; females lay 200-400 eggs. Caterpillar development is completed in about 2 months. Caterpillars feed from tubes of silk, which contain particles of food.

Habits. The caterpillars feed on flour, meal, damaged grain, seeds, sesame, peanuts, and vegetable refuse. This moth is common in flour processing and storage facilities. They are often collected in UV light traps.

Mediterranean Flour Moth

Adult wingspan is about 1 inch. The front wings are pale gray with irregular bands; hind wings are grayish white. Caterpillars are about 1.5 inches long and yellowish white to pinkish white.

Development. Eggs are laid singly on food surface; females can lay 100-600 eggs. Hatching is in about 5 days. Caterpillar development is completed in 10 weeks. There are 4 or 5 generations per year. Full-grown caterpillars may be found far from the infested site.

Habits. Food infested includes flour, nuts, seeds, beans, dried fruits, flour, and chocolate. The adult moths can be collected in UV light traps.

Clothes Moths

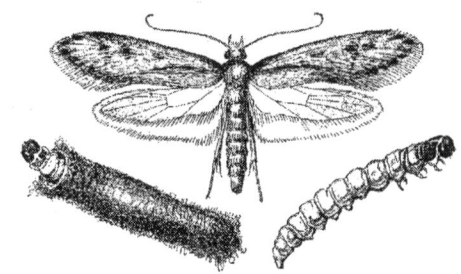

The wingspan is about 1 inch. They are weak flyers and do not move far from the site of caterpillar feeding. Adults rarely fly to lights and are not active in lighted areas. Caterpillars feed on animal horns and woolen fabrics.

Webbing Clothes Moth

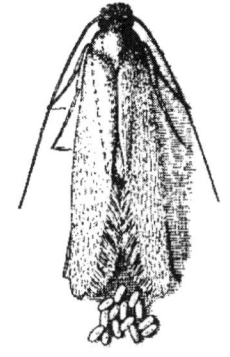

Adult wingspan is about 1/3 inch, and the body is dark yellow to reddish brown. Wings are uniformly gray, and without dark spots. Caterpillars are yellowish white.

Development. Eggs are deposited singly or in batches of about 25 between threads on cloth surfaces. Females deposit 40-100 eggs in their lifetime. Hatching occurs in about 7 days. Caterpillar development includes 5-45 stages (molts), and can last from 35 days to 2.5 years. Caterpillars make a cocoon for pupation. Males live for 13-79 days, and females 10-48 days.

Habits. Clothes moth caterpillars feed on wool clothes, natural carpets, furs, stored wool, and piano felts. The adult moth usually stays in the immediate area of the infestation. They flutter rather than fly in a direct, steady manner.

Casemaking Clothes Moth

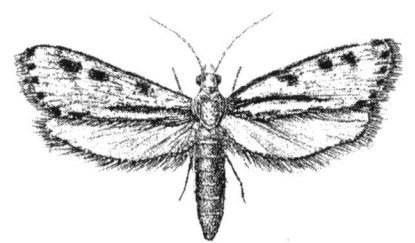

Adult body is grayish yellow. Front wings have 3 dark spots on the middle; the hind wings are yellowish brown and without spots. Males are active flyers, but female moths are slow and relatively inactive. Caterpillars are yellowish white.

Development. Eggs are laid singly or in small groups; females deposit 37-48 eggs. Hatching occurs in 4-7 days. Caterpillar development is completed in 68-87 days, and pupation takes place in the larval feeding case after both ends are sealed. There are 3 or 4 generations per year.

Habits. The casemaking clothes moth will also feed on stored plant materials, such as spices and tobacco.

Plaster Bagworm

Adult female wingspan is about 1/2 inch, and the body is gray with four spots on the front wings. Caterpillars are yellowish white, with dark plates on the segments behind the head; they remain in the case with only their head protruding. Cases are about 1/2 inch long.

Development. Eggs are deposited singly or in batches, hatching occurs in about 10 days. Caterpillar development is completed in about 50 days and there are seven stages before the pupal stage. The life cycle from egg to adult moth takes 2 to 3 months.

Habits. Adult moths are capable of long flights and will rest on walls or the edge of the floor. The caterpillar moves by crawling on the substrate and pulling the case behind. Cases can be found on wool rugs and wool carpets, hanging on curtains, or under buildings, hanging from sub-flooring, and joists. The plaster bagworm requires high humidity to survive, which limits its range to southern and coastal regions.

Sod Webworm

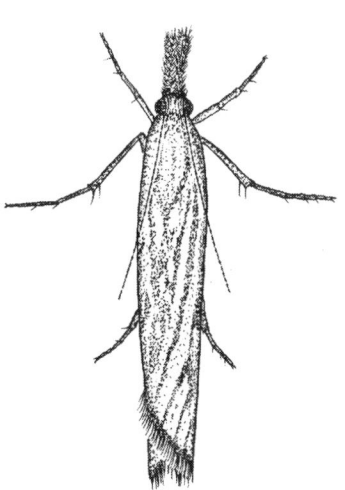

Moths are gray and about 1 inch long. They have long palps extending from the head and long antennae that extended back over their body. The wings are usually wrapped around the body to create a tubular appearance; this distinguishes them from other moths that come to outdoor lights.

Development. Eggs are deposited singly or in batches in turfgrass, the adults typically move in short flights over the grass. The caterpillars feed on blades of grass; the pupa is formed in the thatch layer of turf. Some species have 1 generation per year, while others have 2 or 3 generations.

Habits. The adults are active at dusk and will fly for about an hour after sunset. They are strongly attracted to lights at night and will come to outdoor lights and to windows in lighted rooms. There are numerous species, some occur in spring, some in summer, and some in fall. The moths may be captured in UV light traps positioned indoors, especially light traps near doors and windows. They can be mistaken for flour moths.

GUIDE TO HOUSEHOLD AND WOOD INFESTING PESTS

Eastern Tent Caterpillar

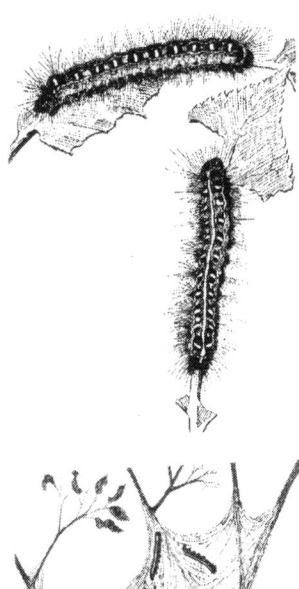

Adult body is yellowish to dark brown; the forewings have two yellowish white lines. Caterpillars are about 2 inches long, with black head and with scattered long hairs. There is a white stripe, bordered with reddish brown and black lines the length of their body.

Development. Eggs are laid in masses of 150-250 that encircle small twigs on host trees. Hatching occurs in the following spring, about the time new leaves appear on the tree. Caterpillar development is about 3 weeks, full-grown caterpillars leave the tent and wander in search of a place to pupate. Pupation occurs in silken cocoons, covered with a yellowish powder. There is 1 generation per year.

Habits. A tent is constructed in a crotch of the tree, and it is expanded with the growth of the caterpillars. Preferred hosts are wild cherry and apple, but it also attacks shade trees and fruit trees. The caterpillars usually leave the tree to spin the cocoon, and they are often formed on the sides and eaves of houses. The oval shape and the yellowish coloring of the cocoon are characteristic of this species.

Bagworm

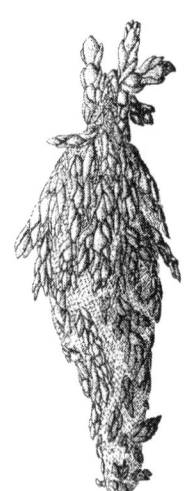

Full-grown caterpillars are about 1.5 inches long and dark yellow to light brown. Caterpillars attack evergreen and deciduous trees, the most commonly infested trees are firs, juniper, pines, spruce, maple, sweet gum, and sycamore.

Development. Eggs are laid inside the bag and hatch the following spring. First-stage caterpillars leave the bag and move onto leaves to feed and form their own bag. Caterpillar development is completed in fall. Caterpillars leave the host tree or shrub to pupate; they pupate inside the case.

Habits. Males leave the case after development, but the wingless females remain in the case. In fall, females extend their abdomens to the outside of the bag to attract males for mating.

CHAPTER 11
TERMITES

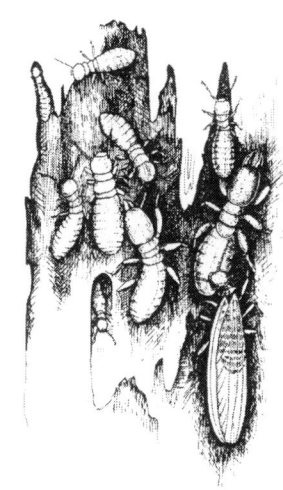

Termites can use dry, wet, above-ground, and below-ground wood for food and a nest site. They live in highly organized colonies, and the individuals in the colony have distinct responsibilities. Workers are small and search for food and maintain the colony, soldiers are large and defend the colony, and the queens lay eggs.

Colonies have a functional male (or king to mate with the queen) in the nest. Mating and egg production in termite colonies is ongoing throughout the long life of the queen. Development consists of a series of immature stages; these individuals develop into soldiers and workers. Swarmers are males and females and usually produced on a yearly basis.

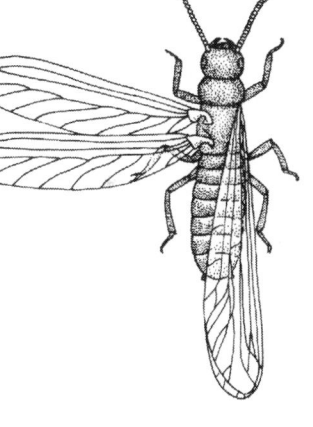

Winged termites (called swarmers) leave the colony to establish new colonies. Swarmers are produced by well-established colonies, and this occurs 3-5 years after the colony founding. The release of swarmers is usually restricted to certain times of the year, and specific times of the day, evening, or night. Swarming is synchronized with regional and local weather conditions.

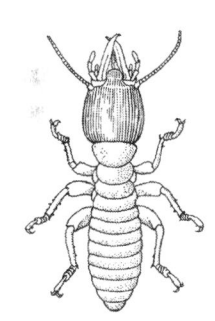

- **Drywood termite** nests are not in contact with the soil and they depend on wood moisture for suitable conditions for the colony. Infestations may be unnoticed because their feeding leaves a thin veneer of wood at the surface. Their rounded fecal pellets are ejected from the galleries, and piles of these pellets are a sign of infestation.

- **Dampwood termites** infest wet and decayed wood, but feeding can extend to sound wood.

- **Subterranean termite** nests are in soil or in wood buried in soil, but they also forage above ground. Secondary nests above ground are connected to the primary nest in the soil by shelter tubes. Infested wood usually has a thin surface veneer.

GUIDE TO HOUSEHOLD AND WOOD INFESTING PESTS

Subterranean Termites

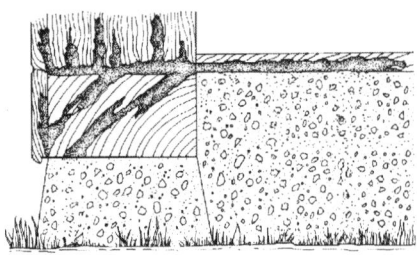

These termites nest in soil, but feed on wood above ground. After many years infesting a structure a large portion of the colony may be located in wood above ground. The Formosan termite is a subterranean species, but the queen may be in a nest above ground.

Colony. Subterranean termites have a colony structure that consists of a number of feeding sites. The traditional enlarged queen is not common in these colonies; egg production is primarily by supplementary queens. Workers and soldiers move between the ground and a source of food in earthen shelter tubes. Most colonies produce several swarms in spring, but swarms may occur in heated building in mid-winter and continue into spring.

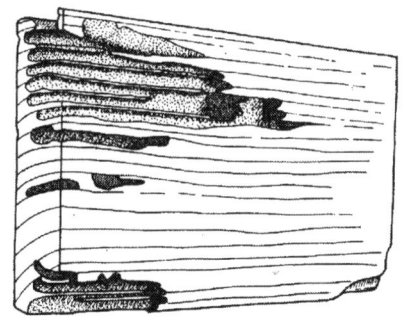

Galleries. Workers excavate galleries that usually follow along the natural grain of the wood. The galleries are lined with a layer of soil, which helps to maintain humidity in the wood. The galleries are below a thin layer of wood and not visible from the outside. There are no fecal pellets in the galleries of subterranean termites.

Eastern Subterranean Termite

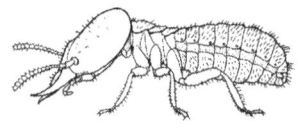

Swarming in northeastern states occurs about mid-day in April and May; in the southeast flights occur from March to May and February in Florida.

- Swarming may occur at any time of year indoors.

Southeastern Subterranean Termite

Swarming is in late summer and fall, usually from July to August. Swarmers are sometimes confused with ants. Pavement ants, which are light brown, often swarm in fall.

Dark Southeastern Subterranean Termite

Swarming flights are in March and April. This is a common species in southeastern U.S.

Western Subterranean Termite

Swarming flights occur during the day in November to January following rainfall; flights may also occur from February to June.

Arid-land Subterranean Termite

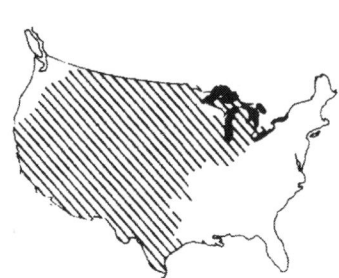

Swarming flights occur in spring and fall; in the central Rocky Mountains, swarmers may emerge in April and February.

Formosan Termite

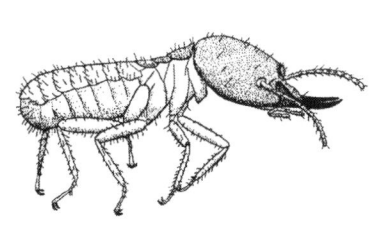 

Swarming flights are at dusk to about midnight, from March through June. Swarmers have a strong tendency to fly towards outdoor lights at night.

Drywood Termites

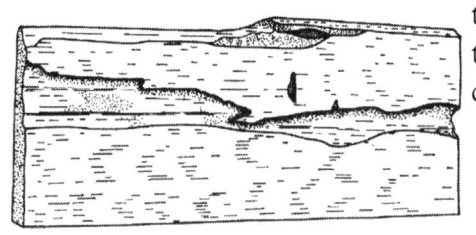

These termites nest in structural wood that has 12-15% moisture content. The colonies do not require contact with the soil, but are able to survive in structural timbers in attics and house framing, and in furniture.

Colony. A large colony may contain several thousand individuals and survive for about 10 years. A typical colony may consume about 1/2 pound of wood per year.

Galleries. Galleries and usually do not follow the natural grain of the wood. Dry pellets are stored in portions of the nest, or cast out through 'kick-out' holes in a gallery. The pellets are six-sided and with distinct ridges, the ends are rounded.

Southeastern Drywood Termite

Swarming flights occur in early evening after sunset in May and June. Individuals in a swarming flight may come to lights.

Habits. Damage is to the woodwork in buildings, and hardwood furniture.

Western Drywood Termite

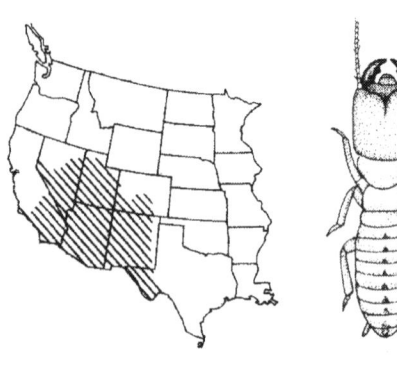

Swarming. Small flights occur from April through November on warm sunny days.

Habits. They infest rafters, ridgepoles, and sheeting in attics. In the living area, they infest window frames, and sills, doorframes, and floor joists. They also infest wooden furniture. Evidences of a colony are piles of brown fecal pellets below small holes in the infested wood.

West Indian Drywood Termite

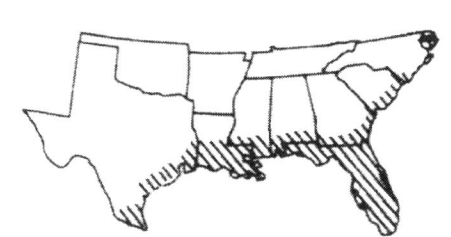

Swarming flights occur in May and June. Damage is usually to floors, woodwork, furniture, and small wooden objects.

Habits. Fecal pellets are small, round and dry; they are usually expelled from the galleries, and collect in piles below infested wood.

Dampwood Termites

These termites nest in wood with a high moisture content, such as rotten or decayed wood; they do not require contact with the soil. They excavate large galleries in wood, and fecal pellets are scattered in the galleries, or discarded through small holes. The pellets are six-sided, but lack the distinct ridges of drywood termite pellets.

Colony. It may take several years for a colony to have 4,000 workers. The maximum size colony for some species is only about 1,500 individuals. Swarming occurs in late summer and fall after rainfall; they are attracted to outdoor lights.

Galleries. The galleries do not follow the natural grain of wood; they are not lined with soil. They often contain accumulations of frass pellets. There are small holes for the fecal pellets to be expelled from the galleries.

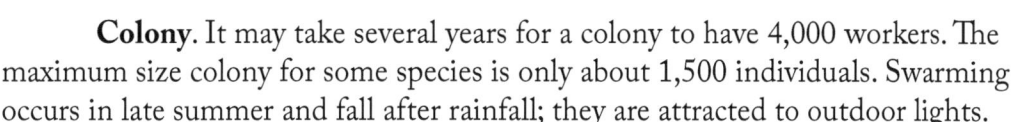

Florida Dampwood Termite

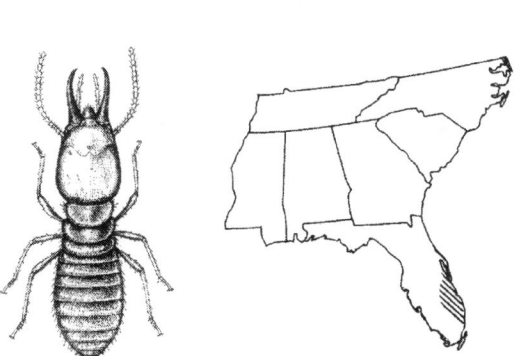

Swarming flights occur at dusk from October through January. Swarmers are attracted to lights at night.

Habits. Natural sites are damp and dry wood in logs of tidal mangrove swamps, or in pine woods near seacoast. It infests wood around building foundations.

Eastern Dampwood Termite

Swarming flights occur in March, June, October and November.

Habits. Natural sites include the decayed wood of trees, and tree stumps, logs, and branches. This termite will infest living trees, including those that are grown as indoor plants for large buildings and shopping malls.

Pacific Dampwood Termite

Swarming is at dusk, usually before sunset, occurs in May to November. Swarmers are attracted to lights at night.

- **Fecal pellets** are rounded and usually the color of the wood infested.

Nevada Dampwood Termite

Swarming occurs at dusk and flights have been reported for January, July, August, and September.

- Swarmers are attracted to lights at night.

CHAPTER 12
TICKS, MITES, SOWBUGS, PILLBUGS

Ticks are blood-sucking parasites of mammals, birds, reptiles, and amphibians. The head, thorax and abdomen in ticks are fused into a single unit. Males are typically small and may be unnoticed, but females often have an enlarged abdomen that is filled with a recent blood meal or with thousands of eggs.

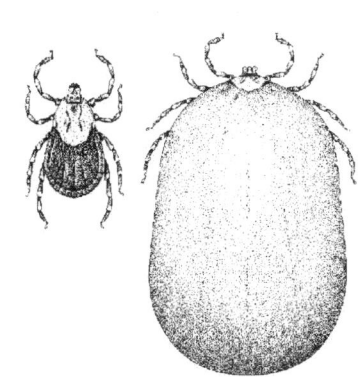

- Nymphs and adults actively search for a host in early spring; females usually lay eggs in summer. Adults search for a host in fall, and small nymphs over-winter and then search for hosts and a blood meal in spring.

Mouthparts of ticks are elongated and project forward from the front of the head. This is the portion that is inserted into the skin of the host animal. It has rows of backward directed spines that hold the tick in place. The rows of teeth are what make it difficult to remove a tick once it starts to feed. This portion of the mouthparts often remains in the skin when a tick is removed, but there are no ill effects from this.

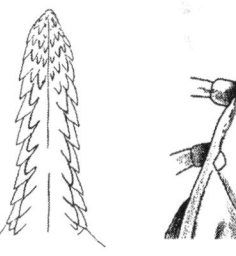
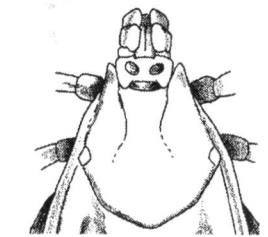

Mites are abundant in soil and many are parasitic on insects and other animals. Others are scavengers on plant and animal matter, and some feed on live plants. There are several species of mites that live in bird nests and feed on the blood of adult and nestling birds. When these nests are abandoned in late spring, or when the nests are disturbed, the mites will move away. Bird nests may be built on window ledges, in the external openings of clothes dryer vents, or other location on the house. When these nests are abandoned, mites may move indoors.

Sowbugs and pillbugs usually remain in damp soil or other moist habitats, and are active at night when humidity is high. Pillbugs resemble sowbugs, but differ in their body shape and in behavior. The abdomen pillbugs is rounded at the end, but in sowbugs there is a pair of pointed tails at the end of the abdomen.

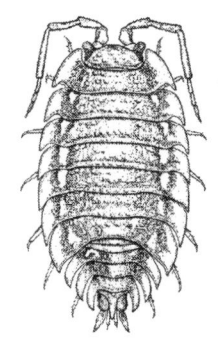

- When pillbugs are disturbed they bend their body head to tail and form a compact ball; however, sowbugs are not capable of forming a compact ball.

Ticks

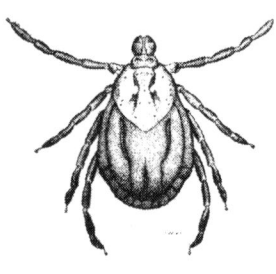

The abundance of deer mice, chipmunks, skunks, raccoons, and white-tail deer in suburban and urban areas has spread ticks to these habitats. Ticks take a blood meal from a variety of animals, including dogs, cats, and people. Their small size and undetectable bite makes them difficult to prevent and control.

Life history. Ticks get a blood meal from three separate warm-blooded animals. Each stage remains on the host for 1-3 days and takes one blood meal.

Eggs are laid on the ground; the female deposit thousands of eggs at one time.

First stage ticks (called seed ticks) find and feed on the <u>first</u> <u>host</u> it can find. Seed ticks drops to the ground after feeding and molts to the next stage.

Second stage ticks feed on a <u>second</u> <u>host</u>, which is usually a larger animal, such as a dog or cat. This tick drops to the ground after feeding and molts to the adult stage.

Adult ticks feed and mate on a <u>third</u> <u>host</u>, which is usually a large animal, including people. After feeding the adult drops off the host. The female lays eggs soon after she leaves the last host.

Disease. Tick-borne diseases include Rocky Mountain spotted fever and Lyme disease. Several species of ticks occur in urban and suburban areas and use domestic and wild animals as hosts. Rocky Mountain spotted fever is widely distributed, and in spite of its name, this disease is prevalent in eastern United States.

Lyme disease is the most common illness carried by ticks in the U.S. Lyme disease affects the joints, heart, and nervous system of people. It is difficult to diagnose. This disease is transmitted to people when they are bitten by the nymph stage of deer ticks. The primary sources of the disease are deer mice and chipmunks in urban and suburban habitats. They are infected but not harmed by the bacteria.

The immature stages of deer ticks that feed on these small animals become infected, and transmit the disease bacteria to people (and dogs and cats) when they are biting and taking a blood meal. Immature deer ticks are very small and difficult to see, so they can go undetected when on a host. Adult deer ticks do not transmit the disease.

Chapter 12: TICKS, MITES, SOWBUGS

Lone Star Tick

Males are uniformly light brown to brown. Females have a pale white spot at the middle of their back. This white spot is the origin of their common name.

Habits. Immature stages crawl to the top of grass stems and other vegetation and from there attach to host animals. Adults and immatures over-winter in soil and leaf litter.

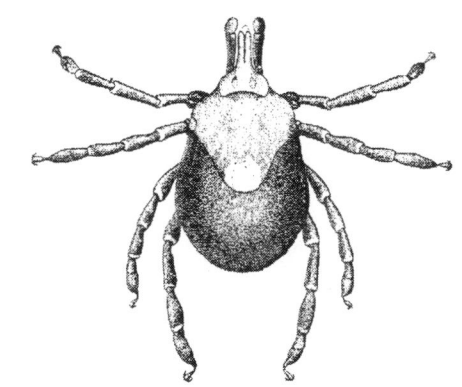

American Dog Tick

Males have an irregular pattern of white marks on their back. These marking are easily seen on the males, but the females have a swollen abdomen and the white marking are hidden. The abdomen of the female may be grayish blue, and sometimes slightly green.

Habits. Immatures feed on mice and voles. Adults feed on dogs and other large animals, including humans. Female ticks engorge in 6-13 days. Unfed adults live for about 2 years. This tick is most common in spring and fall, but they attach and feed on animals in winter.

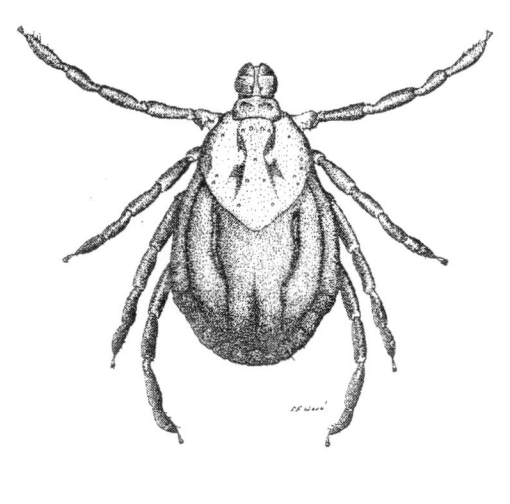

Brown Dog Tick

Males are uniformly reddish brown; engorged female body is grayish blue to light green.

Habits. Immatures crawl on walls indoors, and attach to pets and people; they can survive about 8 months without food. Nymphs feed for about 6 days then drop off the host and molt to adults in 12 - 29 days. Adults attach to dogs or other animals, and suck blood for 6-50 days. Development from egg to adult is completed in about 2 months.

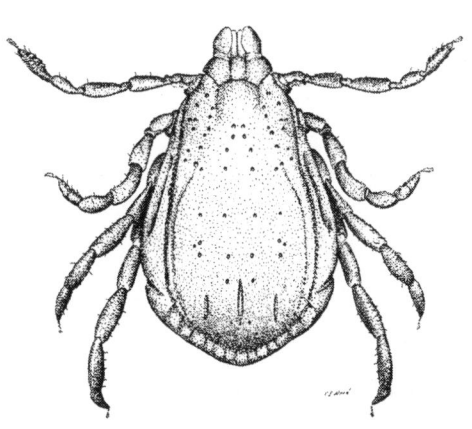

Deer Tick

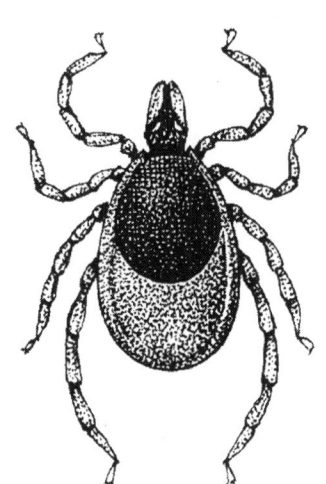

Body is uniformly brown and has a dark brown to black dorsal plate. The dorsal plate of the male nearly covers the abdomen, but it is small in the female. This species feeds on birds, small and large mammals, and humans.

Immature stages commonly feed on deer mice, which is the primary reservoir for Lyme disease in northeastern U.S. Lyme disease is transmitted from mouse to mouse and mouse to man by the immature stages of deer ticks.

Adults attach to white-tail deer for over-wintering. The adults do not move from host to host. Adult ticks do <u>not</u> transmit Lyme disease.

Mites

The body of mites is generally oval with little differentiation of the two body regions. Mites are abundant in soil, water (fresh and salt), and many are parasitic on insects. There are numerous species that are associated with stored food products or flour. Clover mites live and feed on plants outdoors. Population increases of this mite can make it an indoor invader. Chiggers are the immature stage of a mite; they can cause skin irritations when they attack humans.

Clover Mite

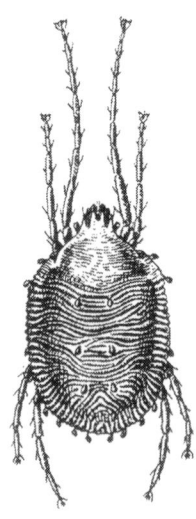

Body color reddish brown to dark green. Front legs are longer than the body. Females lay about 70 eggs, which are bright red. Development from egg to adult takes about 30 days. Eggs laid in late fall hatch the following spring.

Immature stages are typically bright red. They are active in turfgrass and low vegetation where they feed on plant sap.

Adults are active in eastern U.S. from October until May. They sometimes occur in large numbers on the sunny sides of buildings.

Habits. These mites climb on the outside of buildings and enter through windows and doors. Clover mites often occur in new lawns or recently established turfgrass.

Chigger, Redbug

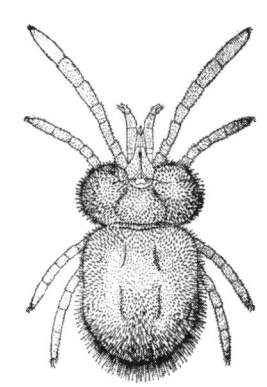

Body of the adult is bright red (redbug), and has a velvety appearance. Females lay about 7 eggs per day in soil, hatching occurs in about 6 days. Development from egg to adult takes about 1 month.

Immature stages do not burrow into the skin (contrary to popular belief), but they attach to the base of a hair. They slowly move into the skin along the base of the hair follicle. Chiggers do not suck blood, but they inject saliva that breaks down cells. The action of this digestive fluid causes irritation and itching.

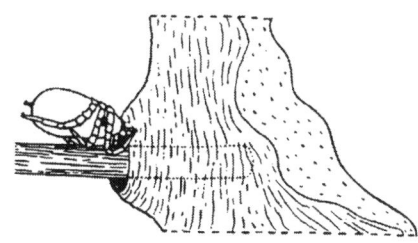

Adults are free living (not parasitic); they over-winter in the soil. There are 1 or 2 generations per year.

Habits. Chigger bites affect people during the summer months. People walking in tall grass and low vegetation may be attacked and suffer itching for hours to several days.

Bird Mites

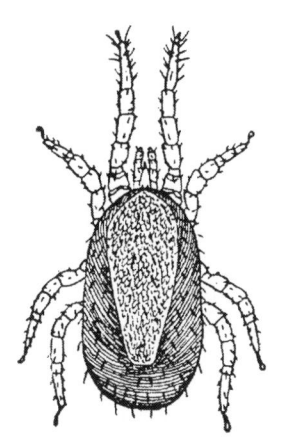

Adults are barely visible to the naked eye. Unless they are moving, they are extremely difficult to see. The color is translucent white, after a blood meal they are reddish brown.

Immature stages can complete development in about 12 days. This short life cycle results in large populations in bird nests during spring when they are attacking young birds.

Habits. When the number of mites in the nest becomes too large, or when the young birds leave the nest, these mites will migrate away from the nest. This migration can result in mites entering buildings, especially when nests are located near windows or vents. Bird mite infestations occur during late spring to early summer when bird nests are being abandoned by the young birds.

Bites. Bird mites indoors may crawl onto the skin and try to bite, but they can not break the skin and feed on humans. However, people may develop a rash or itching at the site of the bite.

Imaginary Mites

Delusory parasitosis is the condition in which individuals believe they are being bitten by something, and it is usually considered to be mites. The typical conditions include something crawling on their skin and being stung or bitten. The cause of this is often described as something very small, black and white, and sometimes V shaped. Frequently these individuals use tape to try to capture or remove these mites from their skin.

Habits. These creatures are believed to be living or hiding in a variety of household materials, including clothes, bedding, furniture, and other items. Usually the problem is only at home, but sometimes it is thought to be at a workplace.

Doctors, including dermatologists and psychiatrists regard the belief that there is a pathogenic infestation in spite of no medical evidence, as a form of delusional infestation.

Sowbugs, Pillbugs

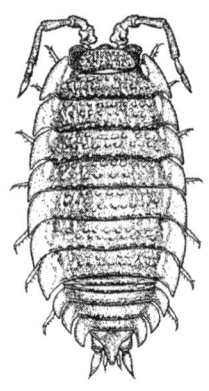 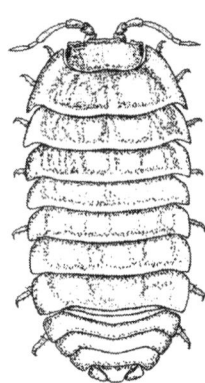

Body is brown and uniformly smooth and glossy. There is some gray to dark gray patches and there are 2 pale longitudinal lines. They have well-developed eyes.

Eggs are retained in a brood pouch; hatching occurs in about 50 days. The number of young in each brood ranges from 24 to 88.

Immature stages and adults feed at night on decaying plant material, but they will attack tender plants.

Adults live about 2 years; there are 1 to 3 generations per year.

Identification. Abdomen in sowbugs ends with two pointed tails; the abdomen in pillbugs is rounded and without tail-like projections. Pillbugs roll into a compact ball when disturbed, sowbugs do not.

CHAPTER 13
SPIDERS, CENTIPEDES, MILLIPEDES

Spiders have two body regions: the cephalothorax and abdomen, while insects have three regions: head, thorax, and abdomen. Spiders breathe through two pair of lungs that open on the underside of their abdomen.

Spiders are predators of insects, sowbugs, and even other spiders. Some hunt during the day, some hunt at night; some spiders specialize in capturing crawling insects, others in those that fly. Most spiders can deliver a poisonous bite, but few of them have mandibles that can penetrate human skin, and when they do the venom is usually harmless. Spider bites are similar to a mosquito bite: there is a small swelling and itching for a short time.

Spider silk is produced by glands in the abdomen. Spider silk is a protein material with the strength of nylon, but it can be stretched by 31%, compared with only 16% for nylon. Silk is used for the construction of a snare to catch flying insects. The spider remains in or close to the elaborate web to quickly capture and feed on the prey. The most recognized webs are those made by the orb weaver spiders; these can measure several feet in diameter.

Centipedes have one leg per segment, and the number of legs ranges from 15 to 181. The first body segment behind the head contains the poison-claws that are used to capture prey. They are nocturnal and occur in moist habitats. The majority of centipedes are predators of insects.

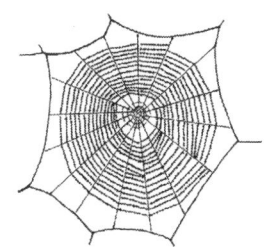

- The house centipede is the most common centipede indoors. It is fast moving and can climb walls and ceilings; it is a predator of spiders and small insects. These centipedes have 15 pairs of very long legs. The long antennae are moved in a whip-like manner over the body.

Millipedes have two pairs of legs on most of the body segments, and they have numerous body segments. They range in color from reddish orange to dark brown and black. Millipedes typically occur in moist or wet habitats. Many species curl up or form a compact spiral when disturbed. Food for millipedes is a variety of decomposing plant and animal material.

GUIDE TO HOUSEHOLD AND WOOD INFESTING PESTS

American House Spider

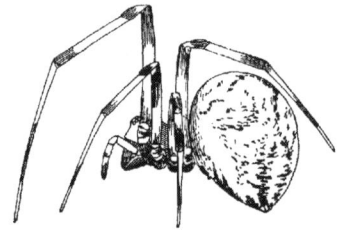
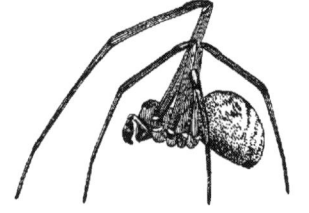

Females are yellowish brown and the abdomen grayish white to brown. Legs of male are orange; female legs are yellow with brown bands at the ends of the segments.

Egg sacs are brown, oval or pear-shaped, and usually placed in the web. Females may produce as many as 17 egg-sacs, with a total of 3,794 eggs per lifetime. Adults are present year round and some individuals live for 2 years.

Habits. This spider frequently occurs in outbuildings and in houses. It makes webs in corners of rooms and frequently in the angles of windows. The webs are easily identified by the long strands of silk that connect a complex web to the surface below.

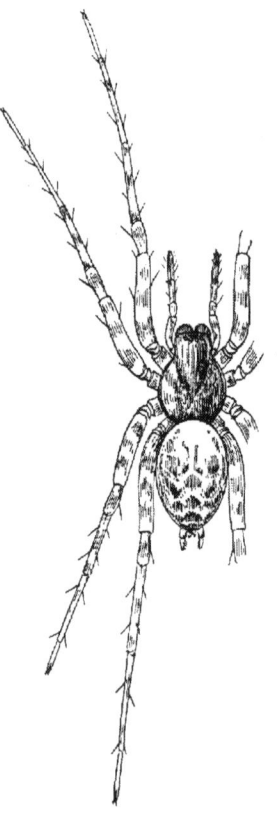

Domestic House Spider

Males are pale yellow and with 2 gray stripes; the abdomen has irregular gray marks. Legs are long and distinctly banded.

Egg sacs are produced through the warm season and they hatch in about 39 days. Adults live for several years, and males and females usually occur together on the same web. Females usually remain at the web, but males wander in the house, searching for food.

Habits. Natural habitats include under stones and in rock crevices. Indoors the occur in cellars, and dark corners of rooms; they can also be common in outbuildings.

Hobo Spider

Males and females have a leg-span of about 1.5 inches. Legs are brown and without bands. Abdomen is brown and white, and has distinct pale chevrons along the center of the abdomen.

Egg sacs are produced in fall, and the females often remain with them through winter; eggs hatch in spring.

Bites often occur without provocation, and for this behavior it is called the aggressive house spider.

Habits. These spiders occur along rock walls, firewood piles, and along house foundations. Males and females enter houses during fall and winter after exposure to cold.

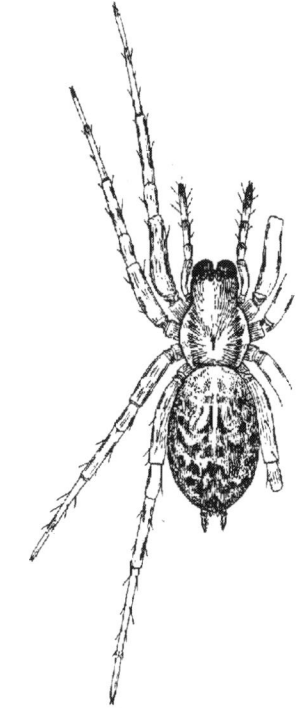

- Although these spiders have been blamed for causing skin damage similar to brown recluse spider bites, there is no evidence that this is true.

Cellar Spider

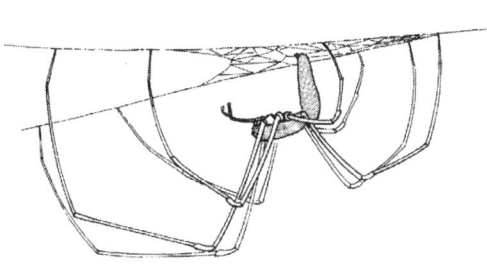

Male and female body is pale yellow except for a gray mark in the center of the cephalothorax. Abdomen is elongate, more than twice as long as wide. The legs of these spiders are extremely long and thin.

Habits. The webs are sheet-like and not easily seen. The egg case is usually carried by the female until it is ready to hatch. This is the most common cellar spider throughout continental United States.

Yellow Sac Spiders

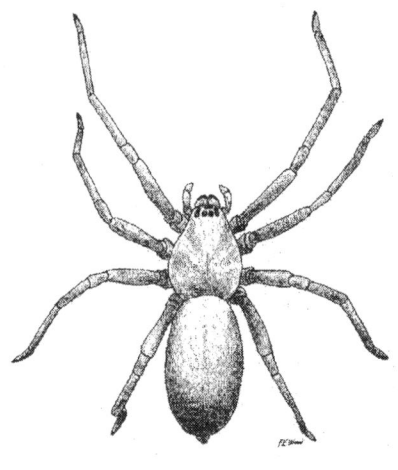

There are two common species, one is light green and the other is yellowish white.

Egg sacs are white and papery, and usually attached to the underside of objects. Females remain with the eggs until hatching. The presence of females with the egg sac is the origin of the name. They are common indoors in fall and spring.

Bites hurt much like a bee or wasp sting. Following the bite there is redness of the skin, itching, and slight swelling. These conditions subside in a few days. Although these spiders have been blamed for causing skin damage similar to brown recluse spider bites, there is no evidence that this is true.

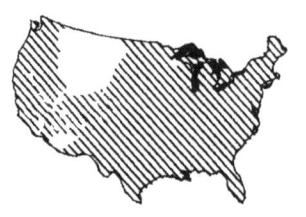

Habits. Inside houses they are found on walls and in corners close to the ceiling; they drop from ceilings on silk threads.

Woodlouse Spider

The body and legs are reddish orange to brown, the abdomen is cream white. The body has few setae. The fangs are shiny and project forward.

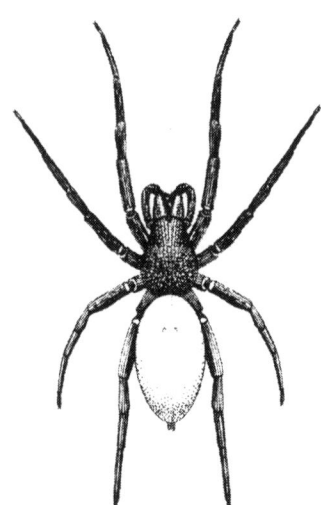

Eggs sacs are light and nearly transparent. These spiders live in a flattened, oval retreat; they hunt their prey from the retreat.

Habits. They prey on sowbugs. Natural habitats include under stones and in rock crevices; they prefer dark and humid habitats. They can be numerous indoors, along baseboards in ground level rooms.

Orb Weaver Spiders

These are large and brightly colored spiders that build large orb-shaped webs outdoors. Most of the species construct a web in the shape of an orb. Females build a hiding place that is separate from the large web or remain in the center of the web, hanging head downward waiting for their prey. The webs are often located on shrubs around houses and close to outdoor lights. Some species only build webs at night and take them down during the day.

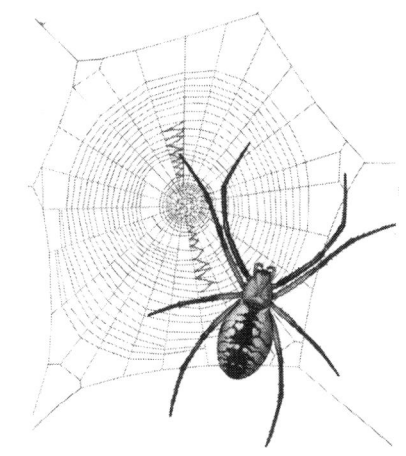

Black and Yellow Garden Spider

Female abdomen is marked with black and bright yellow, or orange. The abdomen is slightly pointed at the end and curved at the sides to form a hump on each side. Front legs entirely black, others with reddish brown or yellow markings, and the other segments black.

Egg sacs are light brown spheres and are placed at the edge of the web.

Habits. Webs are often constructed near outdoor lights in locations such as on porches or garden furniture. Webs often contain a zig-zag of thick silk, which extends above and below the center of the web.

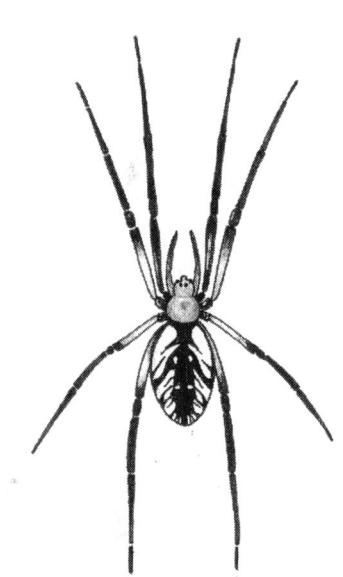

Daddy Longlegs

Body is composed of one segment. The body is suspended above the very long legs.

Habits. They drink frequently and must have water available. They are nocturnal but can be active on cloudy days and dark areas. They eat insects, especially aphids and mites.

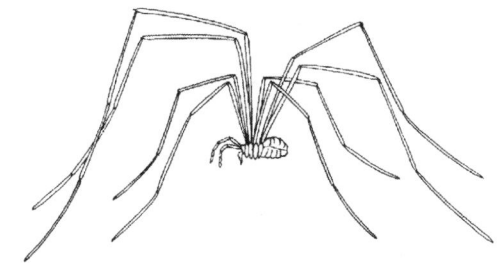

- They are misidentified as poisonous spiders, but they are not spiders and can not bite.

GUIDE TO HOUSEHOLD AND WOOD INFESTING PESTS

Wolf Spiders

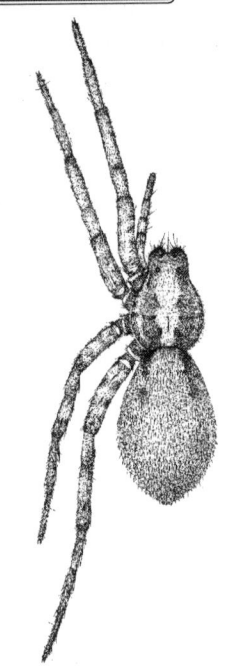

The color and markings of these spiders is variable. Generally they have a large body and long legs. The species that occur indoors are usually 'hairy' and some have markings that resemble the brown recluse spider.

Egg sacs will not be found because the female carries the egg sac until it hatches. The small spiders may cling to the female for a few days before dispersing.

Habits. These spiders do not build a web to catch their prey or to hold the egg sacs, they move around and hunt for their food. They are called wolf spiders because of their wandering and hunting behavior. Most species are active at night.

They are common indoors in spring and fall. In the spring they are searching for mates and in fall they are retreating from cold temperatures. Wolf spiders are not aggressive and usually hunt and hide under objects. They typically remain at floor level, they are not good climbers.

Carolina Wolf Spider

The body is uniformly dark brown and without distinct marking. The underside of the body is darker than the top and almost black, with white markings at the base of the legs.

This is one of the largest spiders in North America. It occurs indoors in humid habitats, such as bathrooms and basements.

Brown Recluse Spider

Male and female (at left) body is brown, except for a violin-shaped mark in the middle of the cephalothorax, with the neck of the violin directed backwards. Legs are long, and twice the body length.

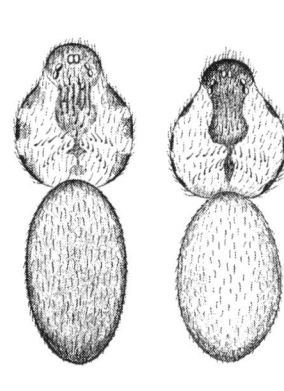
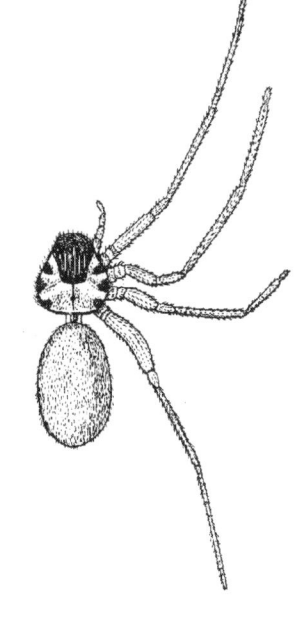

Egg sacs are produced in May to July, with few in August and none in the cold months. Females produce about 5 egg sacs in their life time, with about 51 eggs each. Adult males and females live 1-2 years.

Bites from these spiders produce mild to sever pain within 2-8 hours. At the site of the bite, an open ulcer develops in 7-14 days and persists for 2-3 weeks. The bite from a recluse spider may result in a large wound and a lasting scar.

Habits. They occur indoors and around houses, sheds, and outbuildings.

Jumping Spiders

Female body is black anteriorly and brown posteriorly, and has a pale white median stripe; male cephalothorax has lateral white stripes. Abdomen is black and the middle and lateral stripes are white.

Habits. This species occurs primarily indoors, outdoor populations are not common. It feeds on a variety of arthropods, including the German cockroach.

GUIDE TO HOUSEHOLD AND WOOD INFESTING PESTS

Black Widow Spider

Females are shiny black and the abdomen is rounded. There is a red double-triangle or hourglass mark, or a similar red mark, on the underside.

Egg sacs are globular, and placed in the web. Females produce about 10 egg-sacs. The total egg production may exceed 2,500. Immature spiders over-winter and become adults the following year. Males live 28-40 days and females live 1-2 years.

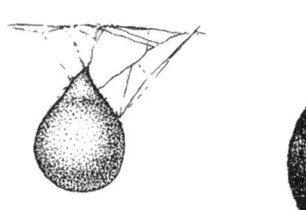

Bites are painful at the site of the bite. The effects away from the site include increased heartbeat and blood pressure, and paralysis of the diaphragm muscles, which results in difficulty breathing.

Habits. The female hangs in an inverted position with legs extended. Females do not move far from their web. It occurs in downspouts, firewood piles, discarded household materials, and near vents and doors in crawlspaces.

Brown Widow Spider

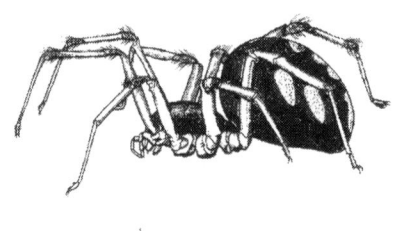

Female abdomen is rounded but not shiny. The top of the abdomen has a highly variable pattern of spots with orange centers outlined in black with a white boarder. The legs are banded and are dark brown at the junction of the leg segments.

Egg sacs are distinguished by the presence of little papules on the surface.

Bite is often considered more toxic than the black widow, but there seems to be no evidence for this.

Habits. Webs are small and placed in well lighted areas, especially those lighted at night.

House Centipede

Adults are about 2 inches long, the body is grayish-yellow with 3 longitudinal dorsal stripes. The antennae and the 15 pairs of legs are very long; the legs are banded with white.

Eggs are placed into crevices; hatching occurs in 30 days. Development is completed in about 40 days. Adults can live for several years.

Habits. This centipede feeds on house flies, cockroaches, moths, and spiders. The long legs and rapid movement on walls and ceilings make this centipede a worrisome pest indoors.

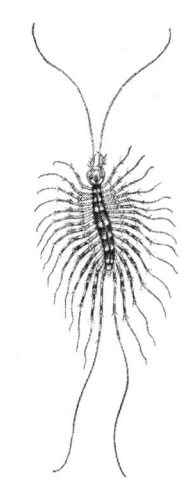

Common Centipede

Adults are about 2 inches long. The legs, antennae, and plates on the body are either blue or gray with a blue tint (Virginia, North Carolina), dull gray and green (Florida), yellowish brown with blue or gray bands (central and western Texas), or uniformly blue (eastern Texas).

There is one pair of legs per segment. They are capable of rapid movement in leaf litter and soil, and will quickly tunnel into soil.

Habits. This centipede occurs in the mulch and other organic ground cover surrounding buildings. It can occur indoors by moving through the edges of doors and windows at ground level.

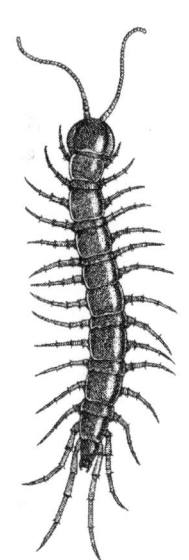

Pseudoscorpions

These arthropods are about 1/4 inch long. They resemble true scorpions by having large claws, but the body is short and they do not have a stinger.

Habits. They are common in leaf litter but also occur indoors or can be carried indoors on clothing. They are predators on insects and mites. They do not bite humans. They have silk glands and usually build a silk cocoon to spend the winter.

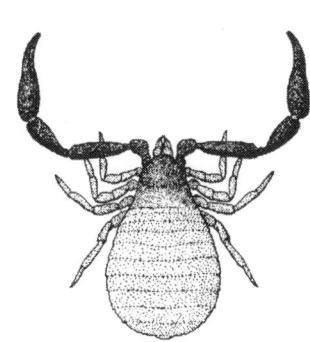

Turfgrass Millipede

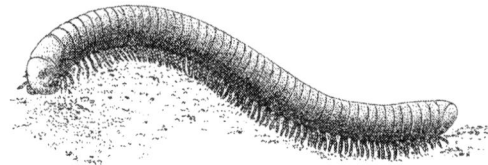

Body is brown and about 1.5 inches long.
Eggs are deposited in the soil, and hatching occurs in about 3 weeks. The number of legs and the body segments increase during development. Most species live several years.

Habits. Mass migrations of millipedes occur as a result of favorable conditions and a dramatic population increase, and then large numbers leave the breeding site. Two pair of legs per segment gives millipedes considerable forward thrust. They can penetrate rotting wood, and the narrow opening around doors and windows.

Scorpions

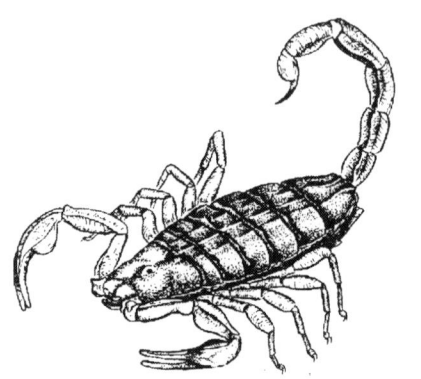

Body is brown and about 1.5 inches long. The large pincers are used for capturing prey. The end of the abdomen is the enlarged segment that includes the stinger.

Eggs are held internally and the female gives birth to live young, which often remain on the back of the female for about 2 weeks.

Habits. Scorpions do not nest but establish a territory for foraging; they may occur in groups in a harborage. Changes in the local environment or habitat may cause them to move into new locations. <u>Outdoors</u> they can occur in firewood and other debris. <u>Indoors</u> they are usually associated with water, such as in kitchens and bathrooms.

Lawn Shrimp (Amphipod)

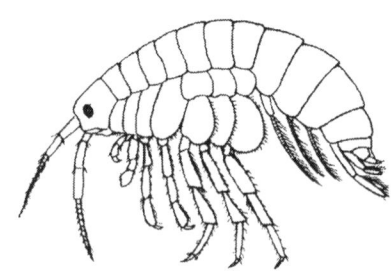

Body is about 1/2 inch long, and brown to brownish black, but they turn red when they die. They are killed (drowned) when their habitat become flooded.

Habits. These are terrestrial amphipods that live in damp soil under dense vegetation. They are able to jump somewhat like a flea. They can accumulate around the perimeter of houses, and rarely move inside.

CHAPTER 14

VERTEBRATES

The most common house-infesting rats are the Norway rat and the roof rat. The house mouse is more widely distributed than these two rat species and more common as an indoor pest. Deer mice invade houses in fall, but they usually do not remain as a permanent pest. The success of these rodent pests is based on their ability to enter structures through small openings and to use nearly all human food to live and reproduce.

Roof rats prefer warm temperatures and occur primarily in coastal regions. Their range is along the eastern and western coast, and through the Gulf Coast states; and Hawaii. In the last ten years their range has been moving farther inland and they may occur along with Norway rats in some locations. Roof rats will nest in above-ground locations and Norway rats at ground level, typically in burrows.

Little brown bats and Big brown bats are common in urban and suburban areas. These bats eat a large amount of insects; a colony of bats can eat about 150 pounds of insects from May to September. Their benefits are often discounted when they are roosting in buildings, and present a health problem because they can carry rabies.

- Bat control or exclusion measures are limited and closely regulated by state agencies. Control measures can not be enacted during summer.

Squirrels can be a nuisance pest in many situations. The gray squirrel is becoming a dominant squirrel in many regions of the country; mild winters and the reproductive ability of these animals have increased their numbers.

- The most serious damage from squirrels occurs when they enter the roof space or attics by climbing the sides of houses or entering from a nearby tree. When inside they can damage electric wires and disrupt insulation.

 GUIDE TO HOUSEHOLD AND WOOD INFESTING PESTS

Rats

Norway rats and roof rats feed on a wide variety of food and can nest, breed and survive indoors and outdoors. They gain entry to buildings through small opening they can enlarge with their powerful jaws. Their teeth can cut through aluminum, lead, copper, asphalt, wood, sheetrock, plastic, and soft mortar. Their jaw can bite with about 1 pound pressure and they take 1.5 bites per second when they are intent on expanding a small opening into a passageway.

Number of young born increases when there is abundant food and harborage. Norway and roof rats are capable of mating and producing young at 12 weeks of age. After giving birth, they can become pregnant again in 48 hours; they reproduce year-round. Their reproductive abilities alone make these rodents a serious pest and make effective pest control critical.

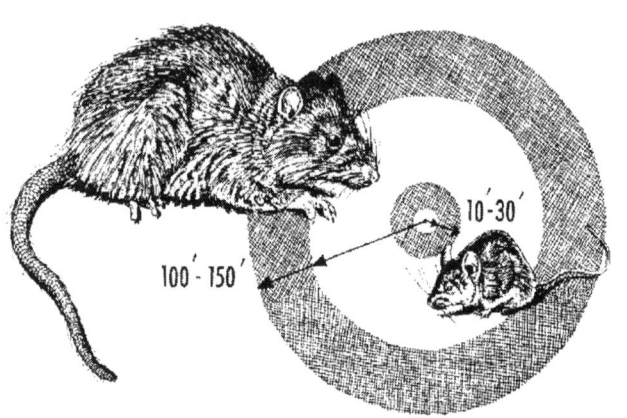

Rat foraging activity takes place soon after sunset and just before sunrise. The *home range* of rats and mice is generally considered to be the area regularly frequented in the search for food and water. Rats have a home range of about 150 feet diameter. However, if their food source and shelter are secure and undisturbed, rats can live for months in an area of 60 feet diameter. Mice have a much smaller foraging territory, generally about 30 feet diameter.

Signs of rodent infestations include evidence of runways used regularly between food and harborage, and fresh droppings along runways and in resting sites. Urine stains along runways can be seen with UV light; rub marks along walls and entry holes are residues from body oil and dirt on the fur of rats. Inspections must be done inside and outside, and always considering that rats climb and enter above ground level.

Rat burrows may be seen along the outside perimeter of buildings. Burrows typically have at least one entry that leads to the nest site, and a couple of escape holes that may be loosely covered with soil. Chewed or gnawed entry holes are usually at the edges of doors or where the siding joins the foundation.

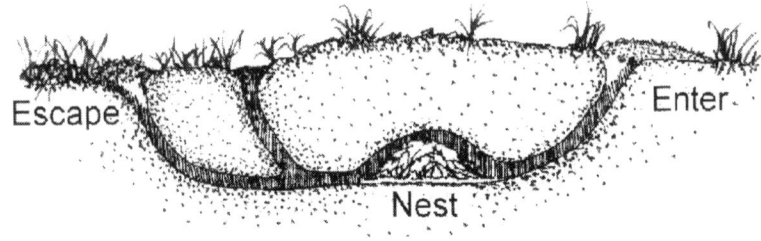

Norway Rat

Adults are about 10 inches long, and weigh about 1.5 pounds. Body is grayish-brown, but varies from grey to blackish-brown to black. Their ears and eyes are small.

Food. They eat about 1 ounce of food and drink about 1 ounce of liquid per day. Their diet consists of meat, fish, and vegetables and grains.

Droppings. Their feces have blunt ends and are about 0.75 inch long; adults produce 30 to 180 droppings per day.

Habits. These rats make burrows in soil; they nest in basements and lower level of buildings. This rat can carry several species of fleas, including the cat flea and the dog flea.

Roof Rat

Adults are about 8 inches long, and weigh about 1 pound. Body color is black to brownish-gray; the underside is gray to white. Tail is hairless and about 10 inches long. Ears are large and cover the eyes if bent forward. The eyes are large.

Food. They eat about 1 ounce of food and drink about 1 ounce of liquid per day. These rats eat mostly fruits, vegetables, and grains.

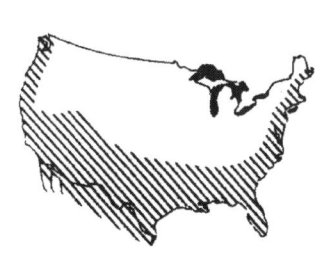

Droppings. Their feces have pointed ends and are about 1/2 inch long; adults produce 30 to 140 droppings per day.

Habits. This rat usually enters and nests in upper levels of buildings; they may nest outside in trees, and dense vegetation. It burrows very little. Activity takes place soon after sunset and just before sunrise.

 GUIDE TO HOUSEHOLD AND WOOD INFESTING PESTS

Mice, Moles, and Voles

The house mouse is a pest indoors nearly any time of year. House mice may remain in buildings for numerous generations and have no contact with outdoor habitats. Deer mice are seasonal pests, they enter buildings in fall when food outdoors becomes scarce and temperatures drop. Moles can be a pest year round, but their tunneling is most often a problem in turfgrass in spring and summer. The system of surface runways made by voles also damages turfgrass.

The house mouse breeds throughout the year; females have litters of 3 to 12 offspring 5 to 10 times a year. Gestation is about 3 weeks. Young are weaned by 21 days and they can begin to reproduce when they are two months old. They live 2 to 3 years.

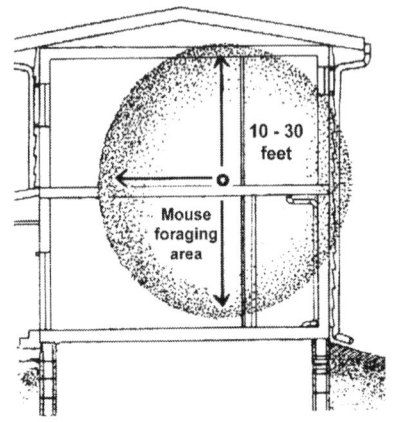

House mice feed up to 20 times a day. They eat grains, fruits, vegetables, meat, insects, but also are known to eat glue, paste, and soap. If they eat food that has at least 12% protein, they can survive without drinking water every day.

☐ The home range of house mice is considered to be 10 to 30 feet when they infest indoors. The foraging territory of mice has to be considered in three-dimension because they will readily climb and move in all directions in search of food.

Moles tunnel beneath the soil surface and spend little or no time on the surface. The Hairy-tailed mole will tunnel beneath the soil surface during the day, but often emerges at night to feed. The exit holes are usually indicated by a mound of fresh or loose soil.

- At the surface moles find earthworms and insects that are food. Moles can be active all winter, but they usually remain in the deep burrows.

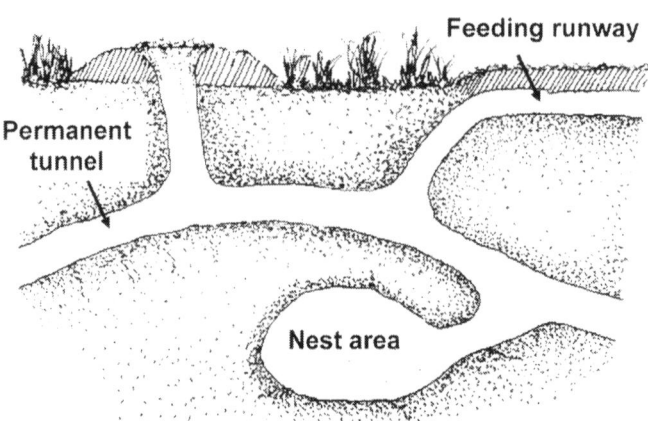

House Mouse

Adults are about 4 inches long, and weigh about 1 ounce. Body color is typically grayish-brown, and yellowish-white on the underside. Tail is longer than the head and body. Ears are large and the eyes are small and close together.

Food. They eat about 1/10 ounce of food per day; water is not essential if the food contains at least 16% moisture. The food eaten includes seeds and grains. Mice visit 20 to 30 food sites while foraging and eat small amounts at a few sites. Mice visit a large number of food sites during nightly foraging and drop feces and urine along the way.

Droppings. Their feces have rounded ends and are about 1/4 inch long; adults produce 30 to 50 droppings per day.

Habits. The house mouse is an excellent climber and can enter houses or buildings from ground level to upper stories. They can jump long distances and survive an 8 foot fall.

Deer Mice, White-footed Mice

Adults are about is 5 inches long and weigh about 1 ounce. Body is dull orange-brown above and white below. Tail is nearly one half the length of the body. Ears are large.

Food. They eat seeds, nuts, and berries. Favorite foods for the white-footed mouse include black cherry pits and the seeds. They commonly cache large supplies of food in wall voids, dresser drawers, cabinets and other narrow locations. These caches can be infested with carpet beetles and Indian meal moths.

Droppings. Their feces have pointed ends and are about 1/4 inch long, they are similar to house mouse feces.

Habits. These mice are active year-round, but outdoor populations become inactive during extremely cold weather. They leave a soiled nest and build a new one in a different location. They will establish a nest in furniture, in cabinets and drawers, boxes in basements and attics, and at the juncture of the foundation and floor joists, especially at the corners. Deer mice will nest in parked vehicles and chew on electrical wires.

Voles, Meadow Mice

Body is blackish brown above and grey below. The head and body length is 5 to 8 inches; the tail is about 2 inches long.

Food. They eat plant material, including seeds, underground tubers, grass and clover above ground.

Droppings. The fecal droppings are elongate and dark colored; they are similar to mouse droppings.

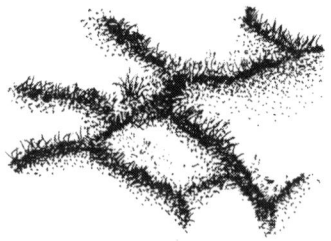

Habits. They make extensive runways below the soil surface; after snow melt their above-ground tunnels can be seen.

Hairy-tailed Mole Eastern Mole

Hairy-tailed mole is 5-7 inches long, the Eastern mole is larger, has a short, hairless tail and webbed toes. There are no visible eyes.

Food. They eat earthworms and insects found near the soil surface.

Habits. Moles spend most their time below ground. Their underground habitat limits the predators that attack them, and populations can become large. They have one litter a year with 2-6 young. Adults can live for 4 years. Hairy-tailed moles are active above ground during the day and are often caught by house cats, and can be caught in rodent snap traps.

Distribution.

- Hairy-tailed mole is distributed in northeastern states, from the mountains of Tennessee into Canada, and in coastal regions.

- Eastern mole is distributed over most of eastern U.S., from the Gulf Coast north to Michigan, but is scarce in the northeastern states above Pennsylvania.

Eastern Chipmunk

Body is reddish brown, belly is pale white. A white stripe on the sides is bordered by 2 black stripes. Ears are prominent. Length is about 10 inches, weight is about 5 ounces.

Food. They eat primarily grains, nuts, berries, seeds, mushrooms, and insects. They cache food in their burrows throughout the year.

Habits. Chipmunks are a nuisance problem. They can cause structural damage by burrowing under patios, stairs, retention walls, or foundations. They may also consume flower bulbs, seeds, or seedlings, as well as bird seed, grass seed, and pet food. They are often infected with Lyme disease and are a host for the larvae of deer ticks.

Distribution. The range of the Eastern chipmunk is from southeastern Canada and northeastern U.S. west to Oklahoma.

Ground Squirrel

Body is brown with 13 alternating brown and pale whiter stripes; length is 6 to 12 inches and weight is about 10 ounces. Each front foot has 4 toes with long digging nails.

Food. About 50% of their diet is grasshoppers, wireworms, caterpillars, beetles, ants, and earthworms. The vegetative portion of their diet includes seeds, green shoots, flower heads, roots, vegetables, fruits, and cereal grains.

Habits. They dig up newly planted seeds, clip emerging plant shoots, and feed on garden vegetables. These ground squirrels will invade golf courses, lawns, athletic fields, and similar open grassy sites to burrow and feed. The opening to their burrow is often hidden and there may be no surface mounds. Burrows are 15 to 20 feet long with several side passages and about 2 feet below ground.

Distribution. This ground squirrel occurs throughout much of central North America, from Canada south to New Mexico and Texas.

Tree Squirrels

Tree squirrels occasionally use house and building attics as a nesting site or for food storage, or they simply enter attics as a part of their foraging behavior. Once inside, they may move into spaces between wall voids and floors. Squirrels gnaw entry ways along edges of attic louvers, or gain access through vents or construction gaps under eaves and gables. There may be openings around the junction of the roof and chimney they can use to enter. The evidence of squirrel activity in an attic includes feces, nest materials such as leaves and branches, and chewed nuts and pits scattered in the area close to the entry.

Gray Squirrel

Adult body is gray above, with a pale gray underside. Tail is gray with silvery-tipped hairs. A black phase is common in northern parts of the range, and there are albino populations.

Food is primarily nuts, especially acorns and walnuts, but they will also eat the seeds of maple and tulip trees. Nuts are buried individually and not in a cache. The buried nuts are searched for in the winter by detecting their scent because they are not buried very deep.

Droppings are about 3/4 inch long, dark brown to black and slightly spindle shaped with one end pointed. There may be pieces of nuts or seeds in the feces.

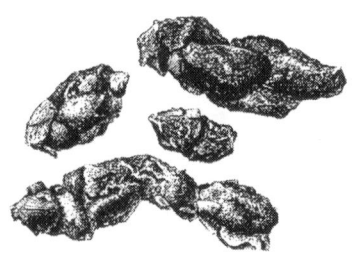

Habits. Adults are active early and late in the day. Mating is in midwinter and a litter of 2 or 3 young is born in spring, with a second litter in late summer. This species does not hibernate, it is active during winter. Young are born in the nest weaned in about 7 weeks, and leave the nest to forage on their own in about 10 weeks.

Bats

Bats usually roost in buildings that are near streams, lakes, ponds. These sites will have populations of gnats, mosquitoes, mayflies, and moths. Selection of roosting sites may be based on location to food and high temperatures suitable for rearing young.

- After dusk bats start leaving the roost and most will be out within an hour. From there they move to feeding and drinking sites. Females caring for young may be gone for only a few hours, but males are usually out all night. Males that do not return to the roost use a 'day roost' which may be a carport, porch, or behind shutters of a house.

Bats enter structures in spring. In northern regions this is usually in April, but earlier in the South. These bats are females preparing to give birth. Baby bats are born during June and July. Little brown bats usually have one pup per female, but Big brown bats will have two. Young are fed for about seven weeks. Bats remain in their original roost all summer. Mating occurs in fall. When temperatures decline, bats leave their summer roost and travel to their over-wintering sites. Brown bats generally live 4 to 10 years.

Inspect for bat infestations at dusk, when the bats are emerging. Bats emerge each evening, unless the weather is extremely adverse. Begin the inspection just before dusk and continue for about one hour after the last bat emerges. The most common exit and entry points are attic louvers, and openings 3/8 inch or larger. Exit and entry points may be marked by smudge marks or bat droppings below the site. Indoor inspections begin with the area around the entry and exit point. Bats roost on rafters and in wall voids and may not be immediately visible.

Bats are protected animals in some states and may not be killed unless rabies is suspected. Live removal of bats through exclusion is usually the only method allowed. Some states require exclusion and sealing of entrance holes be done between September and February. Bats can not be excluded during summer because there may be flightless young bats present.

Bats can transmit rabies. Precautions should be taken whenever work with bats is planned. The rabies virus is transmitted through bat bites, and through a skin scratch. Always wear heavy-duty gloves when working with bats. Bat roosts that have an accumulation of dropping can also present a problem. The fungal spores that cause histoplasmosis can be present in the dried feces. A respirator is recommended if the feces are moved.

Little Brown Bat

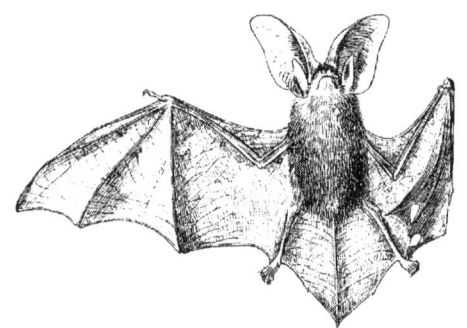

Adult body is uniformly dark brown and slightly glossy, and light grey underneath. Body length is about 4 inches and the wing span is about 9 inches.

Food. These small bats eat moths, midges, mosquitoes, and mayflies in flight. However, there is limited potential for bats to provide effective control of mosquitoes.

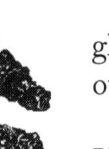

Droppings. Their feces are about 0.5 inch long, black and slightly glossy. The ends are blunt and usually insect fragments are visible on the outside. The feces pellets are easily crumbled when pressed.

Habits. Adult males and females live separately, but come together in fall for mating. This species migrates south in the winter for mating and hibernation. Young are raised in nursery colonies that are in secluded locations, such as attics of heated buildings. Females have one baby per year, born in May to July. Young learn to fly within three weeks and by about four weeks they are adult size.

Big Brown Bat

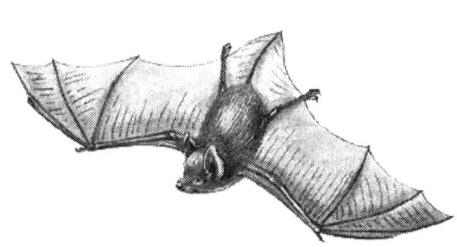

Adult body is uniformly dark brown to copper color and without distinct markings. Body length is about 5 inches and the wingspan is about 14 inches.

Food. These bats eat beetles, wasps, flies, moths, and other relatively large insects. They do not feed in winter but depend on stored fat reserves.

Habits. This species is commonly encountered because of its year-round use of buildings. They are hardy and capable of surviving sub-freezing temperatures. They frequently remain active until November. They relocate in summer if their roost temperatures exceed 95° F. The flying speed is recorded at 40 mph, the fastest for any bat species.

Raccoon

Adult is blackish brown above and with a gray underside. The bushy tail has 4-6 alternating black and gray rings; the head has a black mask outlined in white. They are about 2 feet long and weigh 12 to 48 pounds.

Food includes fruit and vegetables, also insect grubs, earthworms, crayfish, frogs, fish, bird eggs. Around houses and commercial buildings they will eat cat food, garden vegetables, and garbage.

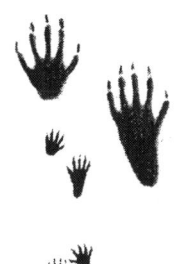

Reproduction. Mating is in January to March. A litter of 3 to 5 are born in April or May. The young usually disperse in fall.

Habits. Raccoons are primarily nocturnal, but can be active during the day. Most daily movements are within a relatively small area. Male home range is 2 to 3 square miles. Raccoons have short life spans, 50-70% of all populations consist of individuals less than one year of age.

Striped Skunk

Adult is black with two broad white stripes on back and extending to the head. Color can vary from mostly black to mostly white. They are about 2 feet long and weigh 6 to 14 pounds.

Food. Adults and young eat insects, especially grubs in turfgrass, earthworms, snails, plant material, carrion, and garbage.

Reproduction. Mating takes place during late February and early March, and young are born in late April and May. The young usually disperse during fall of their first year.

Habits. Skunks are primarily nocturnal, but can be active during the day. They may dig their own burrows, but they prefer to use natural cavities among rocks, or under stone walls, logs or buildings. Skunks produce a strong smelling liquid from scent glands. These glands are located on either side of the rectum. These glands secrete a sticky, yellow fluid, the main component of which is butyl mercaptan.

Pigeon

The body color of wild birds is gray. They have a white rump, rounded tail, usually with a dark tip. The wings have two back bars. The sexes look alike, but the male is larger with more iridescence on the neck. Size is about 14 inches.

Food. They are seed eaters. They feed by swallowing seeds which are then stored in the crop and later crushed in the gizzard. Feeding behavior is to feed quickly and then fly off to digest the food.

Reproduction. Pigeons generally nest on flat areas such as building ledges, air conditioning units or window sills. Most nest singly. Females will lay 1 or 2 eggs which hatch after approximately 18 days. Normal life span is about 4 years.

Habits. Pigeon mites may invade homes from pigeon nests in or on the building. *Salmonella* is found in about 2% of pigeon feces and can cause salmonella food poisoning in man. Pigeon droppings deface and accelerate deterioration of buildings. Histoplasmosis and cryptococosis are systematic fungus diseases in humans which can be contracted from dusty pigeon manure.

Woodpecker

Body is colored red and black, and the wings can be banded. The common species are 8 to12 inches long. The beak is generally long and sharp pointed.

Food. They are primarily insect eaters, and search for insect larvae that may be below the surface of wood. These birds can detect insect activity, such as carpenter bee larvae and adults in galleries in wood siding or other exposed pieces of trim.

Reproduction. Breeding for all woodpecker species is in spring; females lay 3 to 6 eggs, which hatch in about 11 days. Both the male and female tend the young; there may be several broods each year.

Habits. Siding, such as cedar, is attractive to woodpeckers. When a woodpecker is looking for food it will leave several 1/2 inch diameter feeding holes. These holes may be formed into rows, and are often seen near the eaves of the house. One or two larger holes, 1 inch diameter, are usually sign of nesting behavior.

INSECT INDEX

Acrobat ant, 33, 37, 44
Aerial yellowjacket, 52
Ambrosia beetle, 36, 70
American cockroach, 4, 13, 17, 85
American dog tick, 119
Angoumois grain moth, 106
Anobiid bark beetle, 36, 64, 65
Anobiid powderpost beetle, 11, 23, 36, 64, 65
Aphid, 29, 57
Argentine ant, 44
Arid-land subterranean termite, 113
Asian cockroach, 82
Asian ladybird beetle, 21, 79
Asian tiger mosquito, 28, 103
Attic fly, 99
Australian cockroach, 86

Backswimmer, 38, 60
Bagworm, 32, 110
Baldfaced hornet, 51
Bamboo borer, 69
Bat, 141
Bed bug, 10, 15, 55, 56
Big brown bat, 133, 142
Bird mite, 121
Black and yellow garden spider, 127
Black carpet beetle, 76
Black formica ant, 31, 48
Black larder beetle, 78
Black widow spider, 23, 24, 26, 35, 130
Black-legged deer tick, 120
Blow fly, 14, 16, 98
Blue blow fly, 98
Bostrichid beetle, 68
Boxelder bug, 20, 29, 55, 58
Brown cockroach, 87
Brown dog tick, 119
Brown marmorated stink bug, 57
Brown recluse spider, 25, 129
Brown widow spider, 130
Brownbanded cockroach, 84
Bumble bee, 30, 33, 49
Buprestid beetle, 36, 70

Camel cricket, 13, 23, 90
Carolina wolf spider, 128
Carpenter ant, 5, 22, 24, 26, 27, 33, 37
Carpenter bee, 25, 33, 37, 40
Carpet beetle, 5, 7, 8, 10, 12
Casemaking clothes moth, 108
Cat flea, 94
Cave cricket, 90
Cellar spider, 11, 23, 125
Chigger, 121
Chipmunk, 34
Cicada killer wasp, 30, 50
Cigarette beetle, 8, 71
Click beetle, 73
Clover mite, 34, 120

Clothes moth, 7, 105, 108
Cluster fly, 20, 22, 99
Common carpet beetle, 75
Common centipede, 123, 131
Common yellowjacket, 53
Confused flour beetle, 74
Crane fly, 102
Crazy ant, 41

Daddy longlegs, 127
Dark-eye fruit fly, 3, 16
Dark southeastern subterranean termite, 113
Deer mouse, 12, 28, 34, 137
Deer tick, 31, 120
Domestic house spider, 124
Drain fly, 101
Drugstore beetle, 8, 71
Drywood termite, 114

Earwig, 89, 92
Eastern black carpenter ant, 43
Eastern chipmunk, 139
Eastern dampwood termite, 116
Eastern mole, 138
Eastern subterranean termite, 112
Eastern tent caterpillar, 110
Eastern yellowjacket, 34
Elm leaf beetle, 21, 29, 79
European hornet, 51

Field cockroach, 83
Field cricket, 13, 18, 35, 91
Fire ant, 31
Firebrat, 96
Flood-water mosquito, 103
Florida dampwood termite, 115
Florida woods cockroach, 87
Formosan termite, 113
Four-lined silverfish, 93
Fruit fly, 99
Fungus gnat, 16, 101
Furniture beetle, 64
Furniture carpet beetle, 75

German cockroach, 6, 8, 15, 82
German yellowjacket, 52
Ghost ant, 46
Giant water bug, 60
Gray squirrel, 140
Green blow fly, 98
Ground beetle, 78
Ground squirrel, 139

Hairy-tailed mole, 138
Head louse, 95
Hide beetle, 77
Hobo spider, 125
House centipede, 6, 10, 13, 15, 18, 131
House cricket, 91

House fly, 14, 16, 100
House mosquito, 28, 104
House mouse, 12, 137
House spider, 10, 24, 124

Imaginary mite, 122
Indian meal moth, 9, 106

Jerusalem cricket, 90
Jumping spider, 129

Kissing bug, 61
Kudzu bug, 20, 55, 59

Larder beetle, 17, 77
Larger yellow ant, 31, 34, 42
Lawn shrimp, 132
Little black ant, 45
Little brown bat, 133, 142
Lone star tick, 119
Long horned beetle, 67
Lyctid powderpost beetle, 66

Mason bee, 35, 49
Meadow mouse, 138
Meal moth, 107
Mediterranean flour moth, 107
Midge, 103
Millipede, 31, 123
Mite, 120
Mole, 32, 136
Mosquito, 21, 38, 103
Moth fly, 3, 5
Mound ant, 48
Mouse, 6, 9, 12, 136
Mud dauber, 22, 25, 49

Nevada dampwood termite, 116
Norway rat, 14, 135

Odorous house ant, 34, 47
Old house borer, 68
Orb weaver spider, 127
Oriental cockroach, 13, 84
Oriental wood borer, 69

Pacific dampwood termite, 116
Palmetto bug, 88
Pavement ant, 12, 22, 34, 42
Pennsylvania woods cockroach, 83
Pharaoh ant, 9, 15, 17, 18, 45
Phorid fly, 4, 5, 16
Pigeon, 144
Pillbug, 12, 117, 122
Pinebark beetle, 11, 23
Pine sawyer, 11, 23, 36, 67
Plaster bagworm, 109
Pseudoscorpion, 131
Psocid, 5, 9, 93, 96

Raccoon, 28, 143
Rat, 6, 24, 28, 134
Redbug, 121
Red eye fruit fly, 14, 16

Red flour beetle, 74
Red imported fire ant, 46
Red-legged ham beetle, 72
Redtailed flesh fly, 102
Rice weevil, 8, 73
Roof rat, 133, 135
Root weevil, 73

Sawtoothed grain beetle, 8, 17, 72
Scorpion, 132
Silverfish, 6, 7, 15, 18, 27, 93, 95, 96
Skunk, 32, 33, 143
Smokybrown cockroach, 88
Sod webworm moth, 32, 109
Southeastern drywood termite, 114
Southeastern subterranean termite, 112
Southern fire ant, 47
Southern yellowjacket, 54
Sowbug, 12, 35, 117, 122
Spider beetle, 17, 72
Springtail, 12, 89, 92
Squirrel, 32, 133
Stink bug, 20, 55
Subterranean termite, 112
Surinam cockroach, 88
Sweat bee, 30, 40

Tent caterpillar, 29
Termite, 23, 25, 111
Thief ant, 9, 15, 17, 18, 44
Tick, 31, 117, 118
Tree squirrel, 140
Tropical bed bug, 56
Turfgrass millipede, 132
Turkestan cockroach, 86

Umbrella wasp, 14, 21, 22, 24, 27, 50

Varied carpet beetle, 76
Vole, 32, 136, 138

Water strider, 38, 60
Waterbug, 84
Webbing clothes moth, 108
West Indian drywood termite, 115
Western black carpenter ant, 43
Western conifer seed bug, 20, 61
Western drywood termite, 114
Western subterranean termite, 113
Western yellowjacket, 53
White-footed ant, 46
White-footed mouse, 137
Wolf spider, 6, 10, 13, 18, 35, 128
Woodlouse spider, 11, 126
Woodpecker, 37, 144
Woods cockroach, 27

Yellowjacket, 21, 22, 30
Yellow mealworm, 74
Yellow sac spider, 126

Printed in Great Britain
by Amazon